BECOMING MEMORIES

by
Arthur

with the assistance of Illusion Theatre
Ensemble: Michael Robins, Bonnie Morris,
Marysue Moses, Mary McDevitt,
Alfred Harrison and Steven Epp, and
direction of David Shookhoff.

SAMUEL FRENCH, INC.
45 WEST 25TH STREET   NEW YORK 10010
7623 SUNSET BOULEVARD HOLLYWOOD 90046
LONDON   TORONTO

603 10449

IMPORTANT BILLING AND CREDIT REQUIREMENTS

All producers of BECOMING MEMORIES *must* give credit to Arthur Giron and Illusion Theatre Ensemble in all programs distributed in connection with performances of the Play, and in all instances in which the title of the Play appears for purposes of advertising, publicizing or otherwise exploiting the Play and/or a production thereof; including, without limitation, programs, souvenir books and playbills. The names of Arthur Giron and Illusion Theatre Ensemble *must* also appear on separate lines in which no other matter appears, immediately following the title of the Play in size and prominence as follows: The credit to Illusion Theatre Ensemble *must* be in size and prominence 50% that of the size of Arthur Giron's credit, and Mr. Giron's credit *must* be in size and prominence at least 50% that of the size and prominence of the title of the Play.

MUSIC INFORMATION

Samuel French, Inc. can supply the original incidental music score by Kim D. Sherman for amateur presentation *only* on receipt of the following:
1. Exact performance dates.
2. $20.00 rental fee.
3. $25.00 refundable deposit.
4. Music Royalty in full for entire production, which is $10.00 for the first performance, and $5.00 for each additional performance.
5. $3.00 for postage and handling.

Stock terms quoted upon application.

NOTE: Although use of this music is optional, the Author of the Play strongly urges its use in productions.

PRODUCTION NOTES

The play works best on one set, flowing continually, transformations unfolding before our eyes. Simplicity is the key. A few benches that can be moved, a flat trunk that contains props on which actors may sit, and a couple of boxes that can serve as chairs, or, for example, a box for Rosina to stand on in the opening of the play to give the impression that she is elevated on a tall horse and from which Albert can spirit her away. Audiences are delighted when their theatrical imagination is engaged. To date, no audience has had any trouble following the stories.

As shown in the diagram of the floor plan, the set for the original production, designed by David Krchelich, was basically a wooden front porch, with a playing area in front and an elevated extension of the front porch to one side that served as Margaret's parlor and Rosina's attic. Ida's swing in al productions has descended from the flys, which always creates a magical moment. It is useful to have the entire company sit on both sides of the stage, watching the action, or participating as nosey neighbors — for example — opening and closing imaginary windows when Jack first calls on Margaret. If watching characters becomes a visible framework, then it is possible to bring on the grandchildren with ease when they are prompted to ask a question.

Because New York University presented the play in a black-box type theater with a flat floor and the audience seated in bleachers, the scene designer Robert Perdziola created a large, tall armoire on wheels. This became the unit set, which the actors pushed around to different locations. The most imaginative use of this moving piece of furniture came in the first scene, when, turned vertically, with a train engineer aboard, it became the train hurtling toward the audience and Rosina, perched on a flat trunk. The armoire had three doors and the three drawers at the bottom became steps when opened. The doors were used to make entrances and exits. When the doors were left open, it was possible to see characters walking in the distance — the way memory works.

In the proscenium-style Cornell University production, set designer Dick Block created a series of abstract levels and ramps backed by a cyclorama. Hanging in front of it was a three-dimensional, wooden cut-out of towns, trees, and countryside, painted discretely. Depending on the lighting, sometimes this hanging sculpture looked like clouds, sometimes towns.

The choice of who plays what role is, of course, a matter unique to every production. However, the cast lists presented in this script will give you some indication of the most favorable doubling. For example, the actress who plays Rosina has almost always come back as Mary Jo, which gives audiences the sense that Rosina lives on, has another chance. The reason we see the same actors portray members of different families is because I believe that we are all a part of each other. It is important that by the time we reach the Passover scene — usually with Albert now playing Sam, and Jack now playing Jerry, and

Margaret now Auntie Clara — that the audience begins to feel that we are all one family.

If actors can be found who sing and play such instruments as fiddles, harmonicas, or banjos, it adds to the creative climate of the production. However, it is possible to perform with a piano and some percussion instruments. The actors should be encouraged to create such sounds as the wind in the attic scene.

The play may be presented in many ways, but the most important factor is the humanity of the people. One way to achieve a trusting, sharing environment is to use the first rehearsal for the telling of stories about the grandparents of the cast. If the actors can bring in photographs and family objects, this adds to the authenticity of the experience. When this method is used, magically, after the first day, a bond is always achieved in the company, which enhances the ensemble needs of the play.

It is also recommended that the community where the play is presented have a chance to participate. For example, the Pittsburgh Public Theater invited citizens to contribute old photographs of their grandparents, which were then displayed in the lobby. Fred Rogers — "Mr. Rogers" of television, a resident of Pittsburgh — loaned us a photograph of his grandparents. What usually happens — a good test of whether the production is working or not — is that the audience members don't want to

PRODUCTION NOTES
(page 4)

leave the theater, but want to remain to tell stories about their own families. After the original production at the Illusion Theatre in Minneapolis, cast members mingled with the audience and allowed them to talk. Tables with food were set up, "eats" mentioned in the play, such as poppy seed cookies were served. If the production is sincere, it always occurs that first nighters will return, bringing other members of their families.

SPECIAL NOTE: David Shookhoff, who directed the original production staged the play again at Cornell University. In the spirit of experimentation, he asked me if he could try the play without Hannah, wanting to concentrate on four stories rather than five. I agreed. Hannah, easily one of the most beloved characters in the play, did not appear, and, you should know, that the play still worked fine. An interesting side effect of this decision was that Linda, then, became the most independent-minded woman in the play.

Arthur Giron

SUGGESTED DOUBLING

Rosina — Mary Jo, Duck

Albert — Priest, Sam

Margaret — Mrs. Patterson, Aunt Clara

Jack — Judge Patterson, Jerry

Ida — Duck, Fanny Fern

Henry — Duck, James, Stephen or Rosina's Father

Sophie — Rosina's Mother, Angie Roo

Hannah — Duck, Linda, Chee Chee

Little Michael — James or Stephen

Oscar — Priest or Rosina's Father

Of course, the doubling depends on the individual company presenting the play.

The first performance of BECOMING MEMORIES was presented by the Illusion Theater of Minneapolis on the night of May 18, 1981 with the following cast:

Rosina, Duck . . . . Kate Fuglei
Albert, Priest, Sam . . . . Bruce Bohne
Margaret, Alice, Linda's Daughter . . . . Jo Howarth
Jack Sheehan, Judge Patterson,
    Jerry . . . . Michael Moormann
Ida, Rosina's Mother. . . . . Bonnie Morris
Henry, Duck, James, Stephen . . . . Steven Epp
Sophie, Mary Jo, Mrs. Patterson . . . . . . Marysue Moses
Hannah, Duck, Linda. . . . . Mary McDevitt
Oscar. . . . . .James Haun
Little Michael, Rosina's Father. . . . . Michael Robins

In addition to the characters listed above, each actor appeared in a number of other roles.

Directed by David Shookhoff
Music by Kim D. Sherman
Set by David Krchelich
Costumes by Susan Haas
Lighting by Jeff Bartlett

SETTING

The play takes place in various locations in the Midwest from 1911 to the present.

Pittsburgh Public Theater

William T. Gardner
Producing Director

TENTH SEASON
presents

BECOMING MEMORIES
BY ARTHUR GIRON

Created in collaboration with Illusion Theater Ensemble

with

CATHERINE BUTTERFIELD	STEVEN CULP	JACK GRAPES
SONJA LANZENER	KATHARINE LONG	LISABETH BARTLETT	CHRISTOPHER McHALE
HELENA RUOTI	TOM SPACKMAN	PETER WEBSTER

Directed by
LEE SANKOWICH

Scenery by
HARRY FEINER

Costumes by
FLOZANNE A. JOHN

Lighting by
KIRK BOOKMAN

Music by
KIM SHERMAN

Production Stage Manager
ROY W. BACKES

April 16 - May 19, 1985

at the
Theodore L. Hazlett, Jr. Theatre

Cast

BECOMING MEMORIES
BY ARTHUR GIRON

(in order of appearance)

Rosina	LISABETH BARTLETT
Albert	CHRISTOPHER McHALE
Ida	KATHARINE LONG
Henry	PETER WEBSTER
John	TOM SPACKMAN
Margaret	HELENA RUOTI
Sophie	SONJA LANZENER
Oscar	JACK GRAPES
Hannah Carolina	CATHERINE BUTTERFIELD
Stephen	STEVEN CULP

In addition to the characters listed above,
each actor appears in a number of other roles.

SETTING

The play takes place in various locations in the Midwest from 1911 to the present.

THERE WILL BE TWO INTERMISSIONS

The approximate running time of *Becoming Memories* is 2 hours and 35 minutes.

Becoming Memories was originally produced by the Illusion Theater in
Minneapolis in June, 1981.

SOUTH STREET THEATRE

424 West 42nd Street
On Theatre Row, NYC

ELIZABETH I. McCANN, NELLE NUGENT, RAY LARSEN

present

BECOMING MEMORIES

by

ARTHUR GIRON

created in collaboration with
ILLUSION THEATRE ENSEMBLE

with

TERRY ANDERSON	DANIEL KEYES	PIPPA PEARTHREE
ROBIN BARTLETT	NANCY KILLMER	LORI PUTNAM
JOSEPH BREEN	LAUREN KLEIN	JOHN ROTHMAN
DAEL COHEN	KAIULANI LEE	JESSICA RUBINSTEIN
PETER FRIEDMAN	KATHARINE LONG	VYTO RUGINIS
LOIS HOLMES	MICHAEL LONGFIELD	STRATTON WALLING
NICHOLAS KALEDIN	KENNETH MARSHALL	

Musical Composition and Supervision by
WILLIAM D. BROHN

Setting by	*Costumes by*	*Lights by*	*Projections by*
MICHAEL YEARGAN	**LINDA FISHER**	**JEFF DAVIS**	**WENDALL K. HARRINGTON**

Directed by

DENNIS ROSA

CAST
(in order of speaking)

Little Linda/Angie Roo/Mixed Voices . . . . JESSICA RUBINSTEIN
Rosina/Older Linda . . . . PIPPA PEARTHREE
Mrs. Patterson/Mixed Voices . . . . LOIS HOLMES
Stephen/Gang Member/Mixed Voices . . . . TERRY ANDERSON
Judge Patterson/Father Dillon/Mixed Voices . . . . DANIEL KEYES
Fanny Fern/Alice/Mixed Voices/Mary Sue/Singer #1 . . . . . LORI PUTNAM
Clyde . . . . KENNETH MARSHALL
Oscar . . . . JOHN ROTHMAN
Gang Member/Young Lawman/Jerry/Mixed Voices . . NICHOLAS KALEDIN
Little George/Little Michael/Mixed Voices . . . . DAEL COHEN
Gang Member/Mixed Voices/Singer #2 . . . . JOSEPH BREEN
Gang Member/Lawman/Mixed Voices . . . . MICHAEL LONGFIELD
Albert . . . . VYTO RUGINIS
Margaret . . . . LAUREN KLEIN
Rosina's Mother/Clara/Mixed Voices . . . . NANCY KILLMER
Rosina's Father/Sam/Mixed Voices . . . . STRATTON WALLING
Ida . . . . KATHARINE LONG
Henry . . . . PETER FRIEDMAN
Sophie . . . . ROBIN BARTLETT
Vinora . . . . KAIULANI LEE

MUSICIANS

William D. Brohn . . . . Keyboards
Matthew McErlean . . . . Guitar/Banjo
Dean Kelso . . . . Cello
Nina Simon . . . . Violin

TIME: 1911—present   **PLACE:** In various Midwestern locales

UNDERSTUDIES
Understudies never substitlte for listed roles unless a specific announcement
for the appearance is made at the time of the performance.

For Singer #2 and Young Lawman—Terry Anderson; for Stephen, Jerry and Lawman—
Joseph Breen; for Clara and Rosina's Mother—Lois Holmes; for Henry and Oscar—Nicholas
Kaledin; for Sam and Rosina's Father—Daniel Keyes; for Mrs. Patterson and Singer #1—
Nancy Killmer; for Clyde and Albert—Michael Longfield; for Little George, Little Michael
and Mixed Voices—Brian Korn; for Rosina and Older Linda—Lori Putnam; for Ida, Margaret,
Sophie, Vinora and Alice—Lisabeth Shean; for Judge Patterson and Father Dillon—
Stratton Walling.

THERE WILL BE TWO TEN MINUTE INTERMISSIONS

BECOMING MEMORIES is funded by Walt Disney Productions.
The producers gratefully acknowledge their support.

Department of Undergraduate Drama
Tisch School of the Arts
New York University
presents

BECOMING MEMORIES

A New Play by
Arthur Giron
Created in Collaboration with Illusion Theater Ensemble

Directed by
Kevin Kuhlke

Original Music by
Kim Sherman

Setting and Costumes by
Robert Perdziola

Musical Direction by
Brian Russell

Lighting by
Brian Nason

Vocal Coach
Brian Mertes

Stage Manager
Tim Maner

Cast

Genealogies

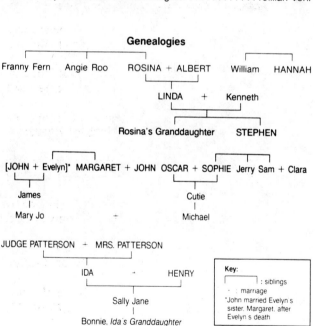

BECOMING MEMORIES

PROLOGUE

MUSIC CUE #1

Blackness. Children are lost in a dark house.

Boy's Voice. Grandpa? Where are you? Grandpa...!

Grandpa's Voice. I'm here.

Boy's Voice. Where?

Grandpa's Voice. It's easy to get lost in this big, old house.

Boy's Voice. I'm scared.

Girl's Voice. Grandma? I need to talk to you, Grandma!

Boy's Voice. Grandpa, Dad said when I was a little baby he found me at the grocery story in a banana bin!

Grandpa's Voice. That son of mine doesn't know anything! You're smarter than him any day. You take after me.

Boy's Voice. I do?

Girl's Voice. Grandma? Are you hiding?

Grandma's Voice. No, I've been here the whole while.

Girl's Voice. Then why didn't you answer?

Grandma's Voice. Because when you call me Grandma it makes me feel old. Why, inside I feel just as young as you, sugar. In fact, once upon a time, I was exactly your age. *(GIRL laughs.)* Don't believe me, do you? Well, I got some old photographs to prove it. Want to see some pictures?

GIRL'S VOICE. Is this Grandpa?!

MALE VOICE. Grandfather?

FEMALE VOICE. Granny?

SECOND MALE VOICE. Granddad?

SECOND FEMALE VOICE. Nana?

MALE VOICE. Were you happy together?

FEMALE VOICE. Did you really love him?

ROSINA'S GRANDDAUGHTER. *(voice)* Tell me the story about when Grandma was a little girl and trapped on the railroad tracks.

LINDA. *(voice)* Folks still talking about that. Well, one day your Grandma decided to go into town, so she got on this horse they had called Blue. I've got a picture right here. *(She strikes a match and the stage bursts into light and color. We see....)*

MUSIC CUE #2, under following scene.

ACT I

ROSINA AND ALBERT (1)

An old photograph of a railroad crossing near the town of Ogden, Iowa, 1911. ROSINA, a pretty fourteen-year-old, barefooted and barelegged, is sitting on a horse. The horse stands on the railroad track and the train is coming!

After a split second, the photograph comes to life.

MAN. Get that girl off the track!

ROSINA. Come on, Blue, move!

WOMAN. The train's comin'!

ROSINA. Please, Blue. Don't stop now.

SECOND MAN. What you doin' riding that big horse, little girl?

ROSINA. Come to town to see the train.

BOY. Look at all that black smoke coming out the engine!

SECOND WOMAN. Flag it down.

WOMAN. It's coming too fast!

(ALBERT, handsome, dashing, makes a bold appearance.)

ALBERT. Give me the reins, little girl.

19

Rosina. Shoo! Stay away.
Man. Get her off the horse.

(Train whistle sounds.)

Rosina. I'm going to die right here with Blue. *(ALBERT jumps on the horse behind her.)* Get off! *(ALBERT, with a whoop, spurs Blue, who bounds off. TOWNSPEOPLE cheer as they gallop away.)* Hey, I want to see the train. Stop. Where are you taking me?
Albert. Back to the schoolhouse.
Rosina. *(Tries to hit him any way she can.)* You nosy Parker, big bully, skunk, slop face—
Albert. Simmer down, or I'll spank you.
Rosina. You live alone, don't you? On that big, old farm?
Albert. And no questions.
Rosina. Put in an indoor commode, didn't you? With a chain you pull down an—
Albert. Hush!
Rosina. It's haunted, I heard.
Albert. Hush, I said.

(Faint sound of train whistle.)
FADE OUT MUSIC.

Rosina. *(Bends close to Blue's ear.)* Go back to town, Blue. To the big train.
Albert. Don't like school, do you?
Rosina. I ain't been there in years. Can't you tell I'm fourteen?
Albert. School ain't for girls, that's a fact. I'm taking

you home.

ROSINA. *(Starts phony crying.)* Boohoo!

ALBERT. Stop that.

ROSINA. Well, I ain't going to tell you where I live. And you can ride around all day like a dumb nut for all I care.

ALBERT. I know where you live. I been watching you girls grow up. Don't see how your papa can run a place, him having just daughters to help out. And you not wanting to do your chores.

ROSINA. Who's been fibbing about me? Shoot! I spend my life cooking for mama and papa and Fanny Fern, and Angie Roo, and Fay, and Beulah, and Lilah, and the whole world.

ALBERT. What can you cook? A man likes to know such things about a girl.

ROSINA. Mud pies.

ALBERT. You're full of the dickens, ain't you?

ROSINA. I make 'em with ayggs. Bet you never had mud pies with ayggs before. *(laughs)* Hey, that's our windmill, see? Wind's really turning it. Come on. *(She slips off Blue.)* Let's climb up. We can take turns hanging from the guide wire. When it's blowing like this you can fly around the world. *(She scoops up skirt, starts to climb windmill.)*

ALBERT. *(Gets off Blue, ties him to windmill.)* Girl shouldn't be letting her skirts blow in the wind, running around without stockings, her drawers showing. You're no baby, Rosina. Good day. *(Starts walking off.)*

ROSINA. Shine! Wait.

ALBERT. What you call me? My name ain't Shine. It's

Albert. Albert von der Goltz.

ROSINA. That's not what the girls call you. *(Takes out licorice from her pocket.)*

ALBERT. I don't like nobody making fun of me.

ROSINA. It's because you're so handsome, you shine. *(Beat.)*

ALBERT. Your horse is probably thirsty. *(ALBERT fingers the many keys on a large ring hanging from a hook attached to his belt. ROSINA is attracted by the music they make.)*

ROSINA. What you got there, Mr. von der Glotz?

ALBERT. My keys.

ROSINA. Oh, let me look. *(She unhooks the key ring and dashes off. ALBERT chases her.)* Lord ... I never seen so many keys.

ALBERT. Keys ain't for women.

ROSINA. What's this big one for? We ain't got keys for nothin' in my house. Tell me what they're for?

ALBERT. Gate, front door, pantry, my desk, my strong box.

ROSINA. And this big, ugly one?

ALBERT. These are for the sheds, and the different bedrooms. And clothes chests, and cupboards...

ROSINA. No. I mean that one.

ALBERT. This key is for the room under the barn ... Pa built for ornery workers, and women, and young.

ROSINA. You mean you got your own jail?

ALBERT. Yeah.

ROSINA. Your Pa put you in there...?

ALBERT. Plenty. When I was ungodly. Depraved. Sure. *(Beat.)*

ROSINA. I can make real lemon pie with real lemons.

Fried chicken and fudge. Suet pudding. And pumpkin bread. Shoot, when Mama's going to have another baby it's my job to take the kids out of the house. Fay and Beulah are in *my* bed, we help pick corn and do the ploughing, and rake the hay. I taught 'em to read. And when they're bad, I put their fingers down a knothole in the front porch.

ALBERT. Why?

ROSINA. Ooh, it's dark under there. Mama says there are nasty scorpions living down there waiting to bite our fingers.

ALBERT. Ain't no scorpions in Iowa.

ROSINA. Mama's from Texas.

ALBERT. And they followed her up here, I guess. *(Lights a cigar.)*

ROSINA. Papa's people are from Denmark. That's over that way.

ALBERT. I been thinking of buying a Great Dane. Either that or getting married again.

ROSINA. I seen you Sundays playing baseball.

ALBERT. You have?

ROSINA. You're a good catcher. Don't your hands get sore?

ALBERT. I like catching things.

ROSINA. Don't I know.

ALBERT. I'm calling at the barn dance.

ROSINA. That's hard.

ALBERT. I like to call out the steps.

ROSINA. Like tellin's people what to do, huh? *(He removes his hat.)*

ALBERT. Come watch me call. *(She sits under windmill.)*

ROSINA. Some of the hired hands asked me to go, but Mama thinks I'm too young. I get so frightened when they come home drunk. Mama puts a knife in the molding of the door so they can't come in. They're sweet sometimes, though. Buying me things from the Sears & Roebuck catalogue.

ALBERT. What things.

ROSINA. Pretty things. *(She lies back.)* Just look at that windmill spin! *(ALBERT can't help looking at her body. She notices, points a finger upward so he'll look upward.)*

ALBERT. Well, I better go. Got my work to do. You're a healthy girl, Miss Rosina.

ROSINA. Take Blue. He knows the way home. Here, take him. You saved my life, didn't you?

ALBERT. I guess I did.

(CROSSFADE: ALBERT changes his hat and becomes one of the Irishmen in the following scene.)

MARGARET AND JACK SHEEHAN
(1)

Up the street comes a rowdy bunch of FIREMEN. A couple of them wear their colorful firemen's hats. They are pushing a tipsy, dishevelled Irishman, JACK SHEEHAN, who wears a mourning band.

It is 1911 in Junction City, Kansas.

MUSIC CUE # 3

FIREMAN #1. "Drink to me only with thine eyes..."

FIREMAN #2. Shut your trap. Want to wake up the decent folk in Junction City?

FIREMAN #3. All cumfy in their warm beds. Ha. Ha. Think of that, Jack Sheehan.

JACK. Stop your shoving. Can't you see I'm a man in mourning? Let me drown me sorrows in peace.

CASEY. There's only one cure for a vigorous man in need of consolation and we all know what that is. Ha. Ha.

(MARGARET, a proud, passionate young woman enters her parlor, a lamp held high. With her other hand she clutches a writing portfolio to her breast. She wears a lilac-colored, lacey peignoir that trails behind her. MARGARET does not hear the men at first, takes out a pen and begins work on a poem.)

JACK. Go back to the firehouse. The whole city could be burning down for all you know.

FIREMAN #1. Who said a fireman's job is to put out fires? You got it wrong, pal. What we like is getting the flames started!

MUSIC CUE # 4

FIREMEN. *(sing)*

WHERE THERE'S A FIRE, THERE I'LL ALWAYS
  BE.

WHERE THERE'S A FIRE, ALWAYS COUNT ON
  ME!

FIREMAN #2. Hey. Look. There's a light on in her window.

FIREMAN #3. I thought old maids went to bed early.

FIREMAN #2. Shut your trap.

FIREMAN #1. Go on, Jack Sheehan. *(They push JACK toward MARGARET'S house.)*

CASEY. A fireman's never afraid.

JACK. I'm no fireman. I'm a volunteer fireman.

FIREMAN #2. Stick your shirt in your trousers. Straighten your tie. *(JACK, staring at the door, allows the men to straighten his clothes.)*

FIREMAN #3. When a man's wife dies, the proper thing is to marry her sister.

FIREMAN #1. Even the Bible recommends it.

FIREMAN #2. Your boy needs a mother and you need a female companion.

CASEY. She's a decent woman.

FIREMAN #3. Pure.

JACK. A prune. That's what she is. Used to chaperone my darling and me everywhere we went — walks, picnics, church socials, hunting jackrabbits — I was in a stew and she was sitting on the lid.

FIREMAN #1. She looks like her sister.

JACK. I'll kill you for that! *(JACK takes a poke at him. The fight disturbs MARGARET'S concentration.)* Never was there a woman in all of America as beautiful as Evalyn. My Evalyn was an angel! *(MARGARET picks up her table lamp and opens the door.)* No one can compare with my wife. And I'll always be faithful to her! Give me your shooter, Casey. I'll put a hole in my head and end it all here. Better in heaven with Evalyn than hell on earth with that schoolteacher.

MARGARET. Who's there?

JACK. Jesus, Mary, and Joseph!

MARGARET. Get off my lawn! *(JACK is pushed toward*

MARGARET and the others disappear.) Jack Sheehan...

JACK. Hello, Margaret. *(He takes off his hat.)*

MARGARET. What's wrong? Has something happened to Little James?

JACK. No. I left him sleeping soundly.

MARGARET. He shouldn't be alone. What if he wakes up crying?

JACK. He never wakes up when I pour whiskey in his milk.

MARGARET. You didn't!

JACK. Drank most of it myself, anywoofy.* Don't fret, the boys at the firehouse are looking after him tonight.

(Sound of a neighbor opening window.)

MARGARET. We're waking the neighbors.

JACK. Let me in, Margaret.

MARGARET. I'm not dressed.

JACK. You're my sister-in-law, damn it!

(Another window opens.)

MARGARET. It's late. You'd better go.

JACK. I've got me rights.

MARGARET. Think of your reputation. And mine.

JACK. Everyone knows you're not interested in men. *(Beat.)*

MARGARET. Wipe the mud off your boots. *(They enter her*

*anyway

parlor.) Sit down.

JACK. Thank you, sister. *(She mimes closing the curtains at the window.)*

MARGARET. You should have made an effort to come to Mass with us this morning. Father Dillon was asking for you.

JACK. Going to church reminds me of Evalyn's funeral. I can't stand the smell of the flowers on the alter.

MAN. I know. *(Beat. She puts a hand on his shoulder.)* I've been praying for you day and night.

JACK. It's a fine thing to see a woman on her knees.

MARGARET. But it's a finer thing to see a man on his feet going off to earn his living. It's time you started working at the lumber yard again. I've bought a brand new lunch pail for you. I'll fill it for you every day.

JACK. How can I go out and leave Little James alone. I can go back to work when I find a good housekeeper. But I can't afford one.

MARGARET. On days I don't teach I can come over.

JACK. I'd pay you.

MAN. He's my nephew. My flesh. *(She extends her hand toward his tie.)* You shouldn't go out on the streets with stains on your tie. *(He helps her remove his tie.)* There was a time when you dressed better than the mayor himself. It doesn't take money to keep yourself clean, Jack Sheehan. Your laundry is ready if you want to take it home. I sprinkled some lilac water on your shirts and drawers. I know we're in mourning, but a reminder of spring will give you courage.

JACK. You look different not dressed in black. Not tired.

MARGARET. I'm wide awake, Jack Sheehan. I haven't been able to sleep a wink since Evalyn died.

JACK. Me neither.

MARGARET. Some lettuce tea will calm us down.

JACK. Don't go.

MARGARET. All right.

JACK. I'm sorry I woke you up, Sister.

MARGARET. I've been scribbling. Poetry is my salvation, you know. *(JACK looks in her writing portfolio, fingers sheets of paper.)*

JACK. I like a good poem. My! Look at all this. And you play the church organ. And you teach.

MARGARET. I'm the intelligent one. Evalyn was the pretty one.

JACK. You look a lot like her. Uh, everyone ... thinks so. You good at lullabies?

MARGARET. *You*'ve got a wonderful baritone, Jack Sheehan.

JACK. You think so?

MARGARET. You stand right out in church and picnics.

JACK. I didn't think anybody was hearing me, except God.

MARGARET. I always heard you. Above everyone else.

JACK. If you'd have me, I'd like to marry you, Sister.

MARGARET. I always felt I could love you, Jack Sheehan.

JACK. Anywoofy, James needs a mother.

MARGARET. It would sure be a lot to take on.

JACK. I could support you.

MARGARET. I've got a headache.

JACK. Got a potato?

MARGARET. In the pantry. *(She sits. JACK runs out and returns with a potato. Cuts it in half with his penknife, presses the potato insides to MARGARET'S temples — a rotary, massage motion that is very soothing and causes MARGARET to release a pleasurable sigh.)* I'd like to be happy. You think you could be?

JACK. I haven't been for so long.

MAN. It's important to be happy. Once happiness gets started in a family, it just keeps rolling along. from generation to generation, like a child's ball.

JACK. God be praised! I've got your word, then?

MARGARET. My word, my hand, my soul. *(He kisses her. To his surprise, she returns the kiss with great passion.)*

(CROSSFADE)

MUSIC CUE # 5

ROSINA AND ALBERT (2)

The Fourth of July. Members of ROSINA'S family scurry in and out.

FANNY FERN. Fireworks going to start!

ANGIE ROO. Sun's going down!

FANNY FERN. No more baseball, you men.

MOTHER. Get all the furniture into the front yard now.

Lots of folks are coming to see the fireworks and they're going to need places to sit.

FATHER. Everybody's got to carry something.

(ALBERT, an unlighted cigar in his mouth, carries a chair. ROSINA carries some pillows. He blocks her path, puts chair down, and lights up.)

ROSINA. Save your matches for the firecrackers.

ALBERT. Want to talk to you.

ROSINA. Not now. I want to get out there before somebody gets the sofa.

ALBERT. Want a train ride?

(She sits on the chair. He picks it up with ROSINA on it and carries her off. ROSINA'S father enters carrying a box of fireworks.)

FATHER. *(To audience.)* Now, I don't want any of you kids lighting the rockets. That's for me to do. Don't want to see any of you playing with matches. Don't want a yardful of kids with their noses blown off.

(He goes off as ROSINA'S mother enters followed by ANGIE ROO and FANNY FERN, who carry things to eat.)

MOTHER. *(To audience.)* Why, hello there. Hope you all got yourselves a good seat. Angie Roo! Fanny Fern! Pass the eats to the folks. Nice of you to come. Why. Abby, I haven't seen you in a dog's age. And expecting again. Mercy me. Rosina, Abby's expecting again. Give her the sofa. Rosina, don't be a hog, honey. Rosina!

(One-half of the company of actors settles down to see the fireworks in the semi-darkness, while the remaining group of actors create rockets and bursting fireworks themselves.)

VOICES. Ooooooh. Wow! *(The first two rockets work beautifully. The third fizzles. Disappointed.)* Ohhhhhhh.

(While the fourth rocket bursts bigger and better than the others, ABBY starts screaming.)

ABBY. The sofa's on fire!

MAN. Get some water!

ANGIE ROO. It's that Rosina playing with matches again.

ROSINA. I didn't do it!

FANNY FERN. Catch her, she's running away.

FATHER. Give her what for! *(MOTHER pulls ROSINA in.)*

MOTHER. My pretty sofa.

ROSINA. I didn't do nothing, Mama.

MOTHER. Give me your finger.

ROSINA. No! I didn't do it.

MOTHER. Spoiling the Fourth of July for everybody.

ROSINA. Don't put my finger in the hole, Mama. I hate it. Please.

MOTHER. You bad girl. Bad girl. *(MOTHER inserts ROSINA'S finger into a knothole on the porch. ROSINA screams.)*

ROSINA. Help! Something's pulling.

MOTHER. Cry wolf all you want...

ROSINA. It's biting me!

MOTHER. It's a scorpion. Bites all bad girls.

FANNY FERN. There's somebody under the porch.

ROSINA. Make'em stop. Help!

FANNY FERN. It's Angie Roo.

MOTHER. Angie Roo. Get out from under there. Let go of Rosina's finger this minute.

(Laughing, ANGIE ROO comes out, runs away followed by her MOTHER and FANNY FERN. ROSINA, crying, sucks her finger. ALBERT appears, carrying a wrapped box.)

ALBERT. Stop that crying now.

ROSINA. I didn't set fire to Mama's sofa.

ALBERT. I know you didn't. *(He takes a hold of her finger.)*

ROSINA. Aouch. It's sore.

ALBERT. My, you got dirty fingers.

ROSINA. Let go.

ALBERT. I've had a present for you in my saddlebags all day.

ROSINA. What?

ALBERT. This. *(Gives her the box, which she unwraps.)* Ordered it for you from the Sears & Roebuck catalogue.

ROSINA. Oh, Shine. It's heavy. What is it?

ALBERT. The most important thing a woman should have—an alarm clock. I like my breakfast on time, same time every day, I'm set in my ways. A farmer's wife's got to be organized. *(ROSINA runs off.)* Hey, I'm not finished.

Come back here this minute. Rosina!

(MOTHER enters.)

MOTHER. Want to thank you proper, Albert. Those fireworks you brought over made a lot of folks happy for a while.

ALBERT. Where's your man?

MOTHER. Father!

(FATHER enters.)

ALBERT. I want Miss Rosina.

MOTHER. Father, you do the talking.

(FANNY FERN, an adult now, enters with ROSINA'S GRAND-DAUGHTER, who clutches a family doll. They sit downstage and watch the scene.)

FATHER. Young as you be, you been married twice before.

ALBERT. Had to bury'em. Sickly women. Rosina ain't sickly.

FATHER. She's full of beans, ha, ha.

ALBERT. She's healthy, all right. Good strong stock. I ain't had a kid yet, and I need a pack of them to help me work my place.

MOTHER. Want some snuff?

ALBERT. No, thank you, ma'am.

MOTHER. You ain't the only fish in the bowl. Lots of boys been courting her, and she's still too young to go to dances. Shoot.

ALBERT. I ain't no boy.

FATHER. He could form her.

MOTHER. That's true. She ain't formed yet.

FATHER. Best marriages is when the man can form the woman to his likes. I formed you.

MOTHER. That's true, I didn't know nothin' till I married you.

ALBERT. Don't want any of your hired hands tampering with Rosina.

FATHER. Had to let them go.

MOTHER. Rosina's working twice as hard now.

FATHER. You sure it's Rosina you want? Fanny Fern and Angie Roo are coming along. Plain truth is, I need my big girl.

ALBERT. I know it's a hardship to lose a pair of hands. You give me Rosina and I'll help you clear up your debts. Maybe throw in fifty dollars and some feed. Truth is, I already paid what you owed at the store. Since you ain't got no sons, it ain't profitable for you to run a farm. Folks tell me you've had a mind to setting up a fix-it shop in town. Well, here's the lease to the room in back of the barber shop. It's a start. *(Hands FATHER the lease.)* Paid up for a whole year.

MOTHER. No matter what I say, Father does what he wants anyway. *(She goes. ALBERT hands FATHER a cigar. Lights it with a large match. Lights one for himself.)*

FATHER. Your Pa had a powerful right arm.

ALBERT. He was doing his duty as a husband. If Rosina, as my wife, fulfills her duty to me, I promise that I shall always do my duty by her. I'm thinking of purchasing an automobile.

ROSINA'S GRANDMOTHER. Aunt Fanny, did Grandma have dreams?

FANNY FERN. What dreams could she have? She turned fifteen when she was married.

ALBERT. Ogden's going to need a good mechanic.

FATHER. That a fact?

(CROSSFADE)

IDA AND HENRY (1)

Eager kindergarten children assemble in their classroom. One sets up an American flag. The children sit on the floor at the feet of their teacher, IDA. It is Appleton, Wisconsin, 1917.

IDA is a radiant young woman with beautiful blonde curls.

IDA. Good morning, children. "Twenty Froggies"? *(The children cheer. IDA sings, accompanied by a piano. The children join in.)*
MUSIC CUE #6
"TWENTY FROGGIES WENT TO SCHOOL
DOWN BESIDE A RUSHING POOL
TWENTY LITTLE COATS OF GREEN
TWENTY VESTS ALL WHITE AND CLEAN."

"WE MUST BE ON TIME, THEY SAY

FIRST WE STUDY, THEN WE PLAY.
THAT IS HOW WE KEEP THE RULE
WHEN WE FROGGIES GO TO SCHOOL."

(HENRY, resplendent in his new World War 1 uniform, enters unnoticed by IDA. He motions the children to keep quiet.)

IDA.
"MASTER BULL FROG, GRAVE AND STERN,
TAKES THE FROGGIES IN THEIR TURN,
TEACHES THEM TO LEAP AND DIVE
ALSO HOW TO REALLY STRIVE.
ALSO HOW TO DODGE A BLOW
FROM THE STICKS THAT BAD BOYS THROW...
(The children burst into giggles and point. IDA turns to see HENRY. IDA is shocked. She has never seen him in uniform.) Mr. Rothman...!

HENRY. Miss Patterson ... children ... I'm sorry to break into your studies ... but, I've come to say farewell. I haven't much time. *(IDA gasps.)* Are you going to swoon?

IDA. It's such a shock to see you in uniform

HENRY. Oh? Am I so hideous looking?

IDA. Quite the contrary, sir.

GIRL. Here are your smelling salts, Miss Patterson.

IDA. Thank you, Cheechee. I think this is an appropriate moment to have our apple juice. Girls, let's show our guest what good little hostesses you are. And the boys will sit quietly while Mr. Rothman tells them about serving Uncle Sam. It is such a privilege to have him here. Say something, Sir. And I shall collect myself.

HENRY. Military training makes a man more orderly, better able to hold his own, a better citizen, and more respectful of the rights of others. *(IDA applauds. The girls crowd HENRY admiringly with glasses of apple juice.)*

IDA. Mr. Rothman takes lunch at the same boarding house where I take lunch and he never puts his elbows on the table. That's the way boys and girls are brought up in Shelbyville, Kentucky, where Mr. Rothman was the pride and joy of his family. Since he was the baby, they tried to spoil him, but he would have none of it, taking himself off as far as he could get to the University of Michigan where he studied Chemical Engineering...

HENRY. I didn't know you knew all that.

IDA. Well, you hardly said two words to me across the table. Boys and girls, Mr. Rothman's father was a Captain in the Union Army during the Civil War. He received many citations.

HENRY. You're a wonderful kindergarten teacher.

BOY. Give her a kiss.

HENRY. I must go.

IDA. God be with you.

HENRY. I do not believe in a heavenly spirit, much to my regret. I have not been able to find any scientific—

IDA. Please. Not in front of the children. *(She leads him away.)*

HENRY. I am concerned about your health.

IDA. I shall live to be a hundred.

HENRY. You're so pale.

IDA. Is it any wonder? I am not so without imagination that I cannot picture the carnage of the battle field.

Please, Sir, protect yourself. At all costs.
    BOY. Give her a kiss. *(HENRY extends his hand.)*
    HENRY. Good-bye.
    IDA. Good-bye.

(After a moment's hesitation, HENRY kisses her. Then he salutes the class. They salute. He goes. A student rings the recess handbell and all scatter, except the two actors in the following scene.)

MUSIC CUE #7
                    (CROSSFADE)

SOPHIE AND OSCAR (1)

St. Paul, Minnesota, 1919. SOPHIE, a Junoesque, earthy young woman is busy making egg noodles in her kitchen.

A drum roll. OSCAR, a handsome charmer, appears. He wears a tuxedo and carries a paper bag.

    OSCAR. Sophie, shake my hand.
    SOPHIE. Why?
    OSCAR. Shake it.
    SOPHIE. What you going to do?
    OSCAR. Don't you trust me?
    SOPHIE. I'm supposed to trust a bohemian drum player?
    OSCAR. Shake my hand. You'll like it. *(She shakes. He winks.)*

SOPHIE. What's this?

OSCAR. Twenty-five cents. *(She tosses the coin back to him.)*

SOPHIE. Buy yourself some real estate.

OSCAR. I'm investing in *you,* Sophie.

SOPHIE. I'm a bank?

OSCAR. Look in my pocket.

SOPHIE. Oye gevalt! *(Pulls out a smashed tulip.)*

OSCAR. You like tulips ... so...

SOPHIE. It's dead.

OSCAR. Well, it's been in my pocket all day. Look in the bag.

SOPHIE. No!

OSCAR. Go on. *(She brings out a pair of B.V.D.'s.)*

SOPHIE. What's this? You want me wash your B.V.D.'s?

OSCAR. No. I just carry all my clothes around.

SOPHIE. Why?

OSCAR. Who knows where I might drop in and spend the night. Don't look suspicious, my dear, just keep digging. *(SOPHIE pulls a chicken out of the bag.)*

SOPHIE. A chicken?

OSCAR. Kosher.

SOPHIE. You pay Kosher?

OSCAR. The Rabbi needs the money.

SOPHIE. I'm not going to pay some shlemiel to bless my meat. Two days I work to bleed my meat. I make my own Kosher. I don't need anybody for anything.

OSCAR. That's what I like about you, Sophie. Proud.

SOPHIE. I paid my way since I been ten.

OSCAR. I know, you walked across Poland, a little girl, all by yourself. Dressed like a boy. Walked across Poland!

SOPHIE. It's not so big.

OSCAR. Look outside the door.

SOPHIE. No.

OSCAR. Go look.

SOPHIE. I'm afraid to look.

OSCAR. Open the door, Sophie.

SOPHIE. I come to St. Paul so Cossacks won't invade my kitchen ... Get out.

OSCAR. It ain't Cossacks waiting for you.

SOPHIE. So who's waiting for me?

OSCAR. Look. *(He peers through window, waves hello.)* For you, Sophie.

(Opens door. Bows low to usher in MAMA DUCK and her THREE BABY DUCKLINGS. They immediately start following SOPHIE around.)

DUCKS. Quack, quack, quack. *(DUCKS discover egg noodles. SOPHIE bursts into tears. Covers face with apron.)*

OSCAR. Stop pecking at Mama's egg noodles.

SOPHIE. Leave them alone. They're probably hungry.

OSCAR. You don't mind the gift? *(She shakes her head.)* Then why the tears?

SOPHIE. Who knows from getting gifts? And ducks yet. *(The DUCKS become concerned. Sit around them quietly.)*

OSCAR. Sophie Simon, I want you to be my wife. Well ... what do you think?

SOPHIE. I think I don't know.

OSCAR. I was thinking about you letting me give you a kiss.

SOPHIE. I don't trust you, Oscar Robins, son of an

opera singer.

OSCAR. Don't you like my tuxedo?

SOPHIE. I don't know why you like so much playing a drum in a vaudeville theater.

OSCAR. It's important. If I don't do the drum roll just right — Ratata-boom! — those poor trapeze artists on the high wire could break their necks. I'm a big man in vaudeville, Sophie. From now on, you sit DOWN-STAIRS. From now on you come with the band when we play Sundays on the riverboats. Ah, Sophie, we'll sail together on the Mississippi, Father of Waters.

SOPHIE. In spring the Father of Waters floods my kitchen. Living down here in the flats, when the water goes up, who gets wet first? We do. Oscar, listen. There's a place I want to live the rest of my days. I seen it. On the top of the hill on Baker Street. It's got three floors, a garden, and a big kitchen waiting for me. That house is important to me.

OSCAR. I wouldn't have to work too many nights to pay for it. Give me a kiss, *then* we'll go look at it.

SOPHIE. Why do you want to marry me? *(Beat.)* He don't even know.

DUCKS. Quack, quack.

OSCAR. You love all living things: flowers, animals. I'll never forget the first time I saw you on the corner of Eight and St. Peter's — proud — pulling a cow along.

SOPHIE. Sold that heifer at the stockyards for twenty-five dollars. Paid five for it.

OSCAR. She's a genius.

DUCKS. Quack, quack, quack.

OSCAR. You're a legend, Sophie. Solid. But you're

single. Everyone knows how hard you worked to bring your brothers over. Your brothers get big, they go away, do big things, and you're too proud to ask them for anything. Sophie, you ain't got nobody. That big house you want, you can't fill a house with memories. We'll fill the house with flowers, and vegetables, and ducks, and chickens, and children. Oh, Sophie, the scent of your breath is like apples. You're so loving and so clean. I'm tired of shtumpin chorus girls. Sophie, I'm tired of sleeping on sofas. I want you close to me when it gets cold. And when we're in our house on the top of hill on Baker Street we will start the breath of life going in our bed. And you will have a couple of early birds for yourself — a little fireman, maybe, Joseph. And a little Rebecca to help you in the kitchen. Then, we breathe the breath of life some more. *(Blows in her ear.)* And we got David. He plays the accordian, and *(Blows.)* Lee on the drums. *(Blows.)* And we are begetting Benny on the cymbals — ting, ting, and Danny, the ukelele, and Sara, strings, and Josh, the piano — and we got a great band going. And THEN all these children is multiplying like the stars in the heavens, Sophie, and we got one hell of a big orchestra! Oye! Children! Grandchildren! *(Does sounds of a great musical finale.)* Do I get a kiss now?

SOPHIE. Maybe. You think ducks like pickle sandwiches?

OSCAR. I love pickle sandwiches. On black bread.

SOPHIE. I think I can fix you up.

DUCKS. Quack, quack, quack.

(CROSSFADE)

ROSINA AND ALBERT (3)

MUSIC CUE #8

We hear ROSINA singing a lullaby. ALBERT carries an unpain-
ted baby's coffin. He lays it down, continues to build it. The
blows of his hammer are hard, slow, methodical.

ROSINA enters wearing a robe, carrying a mug of warm
milk. ALBERT puts hammer down, starts sanding the
wood. Through the following he continues to work
intently.

ROSINA. Albert ... husband ... brought you a cup of
first milk. Still bubbly and warm. *(Wipes her eyes.)* It's a
comfort when the steam from the spray warms up your
face every morning. I hear when you bury a baby boy,
spring harvest's always good. Should have told you what
I saw before the boy was born, sorry I didn't, you expecting your son so many years, should've prepared you, but
right before he come I was milking in the barn and saw
blood in the milk. I knew that was a sign — for all the
world to see. Scared me so I dug a hole and poured it in
and covered it up. The harvest will be good, you'll see.
And I'll make you another boy. I'm on the mend. Shoot,
I'll be ready real soon. Be happy, husband ... *(ALBERT*
stops sanding for a moment.) ... Mama says babies go right to
heaven. That boy was just like me ... *(Touches belly.)* ... kick-
ing and footing. And now he's dancing up in the clouds.
(She goes, carrying the mug of milk.)

(CROSSFADE)

HANNAH (1)

MUSIC CUE #9

A joyful Mennonite hymn is sung by the entire company as a young Mennonite woman, HANNAH CAROLINA VANGGER, appears in a pool of light. In one hand she holds her Bible to her breast, in the other she lugs a heavy suitcase. HANNAH wears a black bonnet and other traditional garb. She sets down her suitcase as the hymn ends, curtsies.

HANNAH. Please. Tis is te office of te new Mennonite Relief Organization? Goot. My name ist Hannah Carolina Vangger. I come from nortern Indiana, outside Topeka, vay outside. My foder, he has a small farm vay out der. Und he always tell us, "Seek not dine own goot, but dat of anoder." You vant me to tell you my qualifications for relief work? I tell.

I finish te eight grade, te time all te girls begins to tink about veddings. But my foder say, "Hannah must got to high school." It is a five-mile valk. I tink te girls out der prefer to get married tan to valk five mile every day. Ven I finish high school my foder he say, "Now I sell te kitchen stove to pay for Hannah's college schooling." Und he give me tirty-nine dollar. It took Hannah four year to pay him back. But I pay him back, ya. So, I am free to go to Constantinople.

Please, I vish to volunteer to take care of te refugees of te Russian Revolution. Ya, I know der are no voomen volunteers permitted. But Turkey is ver te ships are taking te poor Russian refugee ladies. Te Russian troops

45

have treated tem so badly. Does ladies are in terror! I can pick te lice from der hair, give tem goot food, vorm clothes. Some of tees aristocrat ladies don't know how to survive in te real vorld. I teach tem to sell embroidery. I take charge of te voomen und te orphans. Chust a voo-man can do dat. Me.

(A Mennonite man, KENNETH, and his son, STEPHEN, step away from the group of hymn singers. They have been watching HANNAH.)

KENNETH. Your great-aunt Hannah was always persis-tent. Land-a-goshen!

STEPHEN. Why did Aunt Hannah want to go?

KENNETH. Well, son, she knew about hunger. I remember hearing from my cousins how her mother wept tears of thanks when they got a gift of food at a criti-cal time.

HANNAH. Please, I cannot stay in America von more day, knowing America is so blessed vit everything, know-ing te refugees got noting. Te vorst ting in te world is ven you got to leave your home.

STEPHEN. Wasn't she scared? Going to a strange country?

KENNETH. Son, aren't we all strangers in the world? Pilgrims and strangers ... all the time.

(HANNAH is given permission to go to Constantinople. She curtsies, and the singers start another hymn: "Above the Trembling Elements". HANNAH picks up her suitcase and starts for her ship.)

MUSIC CUE #10

HANNAH. Lord, protect me, guide me...

(CROSSFADE)

MARGARET AND JACK SHEEHAN (2)

Whistling happily, bouquet in hand, JACK comes to MAR-GARET'S house.

JACK. I've come for you, Margaret!

(MARGARET slowly descends the stairs, eyes down. She wears a white lace mantilla, but not a wedding dress. In her hand is a single white carnation. JACK hides bouquet behind back.)

JACK. God's loaves and little fishes! Look at the lady. You're the greatest thing since cellophane!

MARGARET. You make me feel sinful.

JACK. I make you feel happy, you mean. Here's your wedding bouquet. *(She does not take it.)* Oh, my ... They are too beautiful for me. People will stare at us.

JACK. They'd stare anywoofy. Two things you can't hide in this world: great wealth and great joy.

MAN. Then I'll put my flower in your buttonhole. *(She does.)* Do you think it's appropriate? We are in mourning. Evalyn hasn't been dead a year. You haven't invited anyone, I trust. You have such a loose tongue.

JACK. You said a simple, quiet little service. And that's what it's going to be.

MARGARET. My, you do look handsome, Jack Sheehan. Indecently so. *(He hands her the bouquet.)*

JACK. For my bride. *(He starts to lead her to the church steps.)*

MARGARET. After the ceremony we'll go to the cemetery and I'll lay them on Evalyn's grave.

JACK. You do know how to get double use of a thing. *(Beat.)* These are pretty flowers, though. Don't you think? John Choo really outdid himself. Artistic.

MAN. So you told Mr. Choo about the wedding.

JACK. Can't keep away well-wishers.

MARGARET. We decided not to include your own son. This isn't a celebration, it's a social necessity. You didn't forget the ring, I trust?

JACK. How could I forget Evalyn's ring?

MARGARET. Evalyn's ring! But she was wearing it when she was buried.

JACK. No she wasn't.

MARGARET. I saw it on her finger when she was lying in the casket.

JACK. When I gave her the last kiss, I slipped it off.

MARGARET. Why?

JACK. It's expensive.

MARGARET. I want my own ring!

JACK. You can't do that to Little James.

MARGARET. What?

JACK. He's going to be carrying it on a red cushion.

MARGARET. But he wasn't supposed to be at the church today.

JACK. He wanted to see his father get married. He's been bragging about it to his little chums.

MARGARET. I suppose they're going to be there, too?

JACK. Only the ones who can sing. The choirboys are going to sing a hymn or two.

MARGARET. What will people say?! We agreed to a quiet wedding. What a scandal! A scandal!

JACK. I know. But I was thinking of you.

MARGARET. Thinking of yourself, you mean. Always want to be the center of attention. The life of the party. When are you going to learn life isn't a party? *(Through the above JACK has started a mock boxing match with her. By the end of her speech he has swept her into the air in his arms. She looks down at him, smiles.)*

JACK. I think I've fallen in love with you. You're a passionate one, you are.

(Bells start ringing.)

JACK. There go the bells. They've seen us coming.

MARGARET. I think the church is on fire! Look!

(Sound of fire alarms, clanking engine bells.)

JACK. It's the All Saints Engine House! Hi, boys.

MARGARET. They're spraying the church doors!

JACK. They're making an archway for us to pass under.

(FATHER DILLON appears, dripping wet.)

FATHER DILLON. Hooligans! Get off the steps of my church.

MARGARET. This is mortifying...

FATHER DILLON. Have you no decency.

JACK. Leave them alone. This is a matter of civic importance.

TOWNSPEOPLE. Speech! Speech!

FATHER DILLON. Jack Sheehan, you're not putting one foot inside this church.

JACK. I helped build this church with lumber from our own lumberyard.

FATHER DILLON. You're creating a public spectacle!!

JACK. Ain't that the way with holy matrimony — the most earthshaking, miraculous, public spectacle of them all? A happy bed holds the universe in place, and makes the inhabitants around it glad. Look at the smiles around you — they know what's coming. They want more peace in the world, not less. And passion is the basis for it.

TOWNSPEOPLE. Let him in ... perform the ceremony ... He knows what he's talking about ... *(Holding MAR-GARET'S hand, JACK looks at her lovingly.)* ... Let them in!

FATHER DILLON. Well, for the sake of peace ... but wipe the mud off your boots, all of you.

(FATHER DILLON goes into the church. TOWNSPEOPLE form the church arch. JACK and MARGARET start to march forward. Freeze. Lights change. They form a photograph. JAMES and MARY JO step forward.)

JAMES. Mary Jo, here's a photograph of my father's wedding to your grandmother Margaret.

MARY JO. Dad, I had a dream about her last night. Was she ever really happy?

JAMES. I think only on her wedding day.

(JACK and MARGARET enter the church as a triumphant hymn begins. TOWNSPEOPLE toss rose petals.)

MUSIC CUE #11
                    (CROSSFADE)

SOPHIE AND OSCAR (2)

MUSIC CUE #12

SOPHIE enters singing a Yiddish lullaby. ROSINA, sitting on the side of the stage, picks up the melody and sings along as she sews. SOPHIE is dressed for Shabbos*, she radiates an inner joy.

SOPHIE. Cutie, you hear me? This is your Mama singing. From the moment the doctor said to me I was going to be your Mama, I ain't been able to stop all day! *(She takes earrings out of her pocket, starts putting them on. Then covers her hair with a lace mantilla.)* Your Papa knows Shabbos* is important for me, so he promised to be here — for once. Oh, he's a generous man, but — Cutie, you ain't been born yet, but you and me, we gotta have a talk. Right now. Because when your drum-player Papa gets word he's a Papa — ratata-boom! He's going to put the Robins

*Sabbath

Curse on you. That's your Papa's name: Robins, Oscar Robins. No! You ain't going to be a dreamer drummer man sleeping all day, out all night, ratata-booming your life away. Soon as I got the news about you at the clinic today, my mouth filled with my heart. So listen honey, this is my heart talking. Son of Sophie, IT'S A HARD LIFE. Got to prepare to make a place for yourself, Cutie. Education's so important. Gott in Himmel! In America those don't got it is always an outsider. But if you're plenty educated, nobody's going to sell you rotten tomatoes. *(It looks as if OSCAR isn't coming home. SOPHIE takes off her earrings.)* Cutie, I think maybe I'm going to have to be a Mama *and* Papa for you. I get no help from him. I married the Emperor of Russia.

(OSCAR enters carrying a painting.)

SOPHIE. Don't tell me. You're sorry to be late. What's this?

OSCAR. A painting of radishes.

SOPHIE. How much you pay for it?

OSCAR. It's a present for you, Sophie.

SOPHIE. Give it back.

OSCAR. I can't. The painter's short of cash. Don't scream. I've had a hard day.

SOPHIE. Yeah, with Janeen the saxophone player!

OSCAR. Be nice to me, Sophie.

SOPHIE. Why?

OSCAR. Life's hard. *(SOPHIE hits her head — can she believe what she's hearing?)*

SOPHIE. What? What did you say? I don't believe this.

You ain't dreaming no more?

OSCAR. No. I'm thinking.

SOPHIE. About what? What happened? Want a glass tea?

OSCAR. Oh, no. You ain't reading my tea leaves.

SOPHIE. Give me your hand. Shake my hand. *(She holds his hand.)* Someone held your hand real tight.

OSCAR. I ain't seen one solitary dame today.

SOPHIE. The angel of death, death held your hand.

OSCAR. You're close.

SOPHIE. You almost died today — crossing the street.

OSCAR. Not me. An old wino. A truck got him. And the poor old guy just lay by himself in the middle of the street. I held his hand until the ambulance came. That's why I'm late.

SOPHIE. What happened to the old man?

OSCAR. Sophie, the old man died. The old man ... he died in my arms. *(Starts to cry.)* Here, read my palm. I want to know that I'm not going to end up that way on the street, no cash in my pocket, with no one to hold my hand when I die. *(SOPHIE takes him in her arms.)* I don't want to die without you. I'm so ashamed of making you suffer. I love you so much. I'm so frightened, Sophie. I always been so frightened of ending up like that old guy without a wife, a family, smelling of piss and booze. A bum. Oh, honey, I'll change, get up early, give up music, get a steady job ... poor old beggar ... poor old grandfather...

SOPHIE. That man's like a brother to me! He caused a miracle! Whatever his name was, that's what we'll name the baby.

OSCAR. What baby?

SOPHIE. Never mind. Give me the name. What was the old man's name?

OSCAR. I don't know. A baby — Sophie, a baby? *(He sings "Alexander's Ragtime Band" as they go off arm in arm.)*

(CROSSFADE)

IDA AND HENRY (2)

"The Missouri Waltz" is being played softly on the piano. On his front porch, JUDGE PATTERSON is reading the newspaper; a group of children tossing a ball run over his lawn and off into the street. A swarm of gnats annoys the JUDGE.

JUDGE. Shoo. Get away. Damn Moose Birds.

(He hears HENRY driving his new Model T Ford up the street. BOYS whistle, react to automobile. HENRY honks.)

JUDGE. Hey! Get off the street, you boys! Let the man pass.

BOY. *(off)* Get a horse!

(Honks. Sound of dirt clod thrown at car. BOYS and GIRLS laugh.)

JUDGE. Don't you throw dirt clods at that automobile! L.C., I saw you. I'm going to tell your pop. Stop that. I'll throw all you boys in jail! Scat!

(Sound of car being parked.)

JUDGE. Hey, mister. You all right?

(HENRY enters, wearing his best suit, carries presents. He removes his hat.)

HENRY. No harm done.

JUDGE. Savages. Don't know what this country's coming to.

HENRY. Farm boy threw an egg at me outside Appleton this morning.

JUDGE. Well, if the kids don't get you, the Moose Birds will. Shoo. Can I look at your machine? I say, can I look at your Ford there?

HENRY. That piano playing's sure pretty.

JUDGE. Don't remember seeing you in these parts before.

HENRY. Well, I've come to call on my fiancée. I've been in the Army. *(Hands JUDGE a card.)* Judge, I am Henry Rothman.

JUDGE. Rothman ... Henry ... Abraham.

HENRY. That's right, Judge.

JUDGE. My name's Patterson.

HENRY. I know.

JUDGE. Who's the lucky young lady? Maybe I know her.

HENRY. Your own sweet daughter, sir.

JUDGE. Alice? No, it can't be Alice, she's not sweet.

HENRY. Ida Maria. She hasn't married anybody else, has she? Is she promised to another?

JUDGE. Ida's not marrying anyone I know of.

HENRY. She's marrying me.

JUDGE. Does she know you?

HENRY. We used to eat lunch together.

JUDGE. Mother!

(MRS. PATTERSON rushes out.)

MRS. PATTERSON. What is it?

JUDGE. This is Mr. Rothman.

MRS. PATTERSON. Oh.

JUDGE. You know...?

MRS. PATTERSON. He wrote letters from France.

JUDGE. Why wasn't I told?

MRS. PATTERSON. You surely were. You got the stamps.

JUDGE. You never said who they were from.

MRS. PATTERSON. I said a friend of Ida's.

JUDGE. Not a beau.

MRS. PATTERSON. Ida's in bed, Mr. Rothman. With pneumonia. She told me she can't see any of her friends for a while.

HENRY. When I returned from the war, I heard she was no longer teaching.

MRS. PATTERSON. Teaching made her very pale, very pale indeed.

HENRY. I never met a girl with more translucent skin.

MRS. PATTERSON. Do you how Ida Maria got such beautiful white skin?

JUDGE. Mr. Rothman isn't interested in that story, dear.

HENRY. Yes, I am. I'm very interested.

MRS. PATTERSON. I was sick the whole nine months I was carrying her. Vomiting...

JUDGE. Mother...

MRS. PATTERSON. ...Oh, so sick, people said to me, you're suffering so much that child is going to be the consolation of your old age. Anyhow, I had such gases I had to take something. Well, every day I took BiSodol mints — you know that white, powdery stuff. I took so much of it Ida was born with the whitest skin in Wisconsin.

(ALICE enters, drying a plate.)

HENRY. You must be Alice.

ALICE. IDA! IDA! *(Turns, runs inside.)*

JUDGE. That girl could wake the cows.

ALICE. *(off)* Ida! He's here!

MRS. PATTERSON. Alice is my strong girl. She helps with the heavy housework. Ida's my delicate one. She does the dusting. She can't exert herself too much. When she came home, Father put up a swing for her in the garden. But even that gives her "Surmenage." Now, Father. Mr. Rothman's been to France, I'm sure he knows what I mean.

HENRY. Uh...

MRS. PATTERSON. Well, that's what she gets. "Surmenage" from the slightest excitement.

(IDA rushes on, glowing, beautiful, a large bow gathers her curls at the nape of her neck. ALICE follows. IDA and HENRY stare at each other.)

HENRY. Ida...

IDA. Henry ... You've come for me.

HENRY. Yes. *(Beat.)*

MRS. PATTERSON. You should be in bed.

IDA. I was playing the piano.

HENRY. I heard you. Are you going to faint?

IDA. Would you like some water?

HENRY. I wouldn't mind your fainting.

IDA. You look so pale.

HENRY. I want to take care of you.

ALICE. He's funny.

IDA. This is my father ... *(Mistakenly indicated her mother.)* ... my mother ... my sister, Alice...

HENRY. How do you do ... How do you do ... How do you do.

IDA. When I was teaching in Appleton, before the war, Mr. Rothman and I used to take lunch together at the same boarding house.

HENRY. I've never forgotten those lunches all these years.

IDA. All the girls used to tease me that I couldn't catch his attention. They dared me to crack his reserve.

ALICE. Ida's blushing.

HENRY. How's your asthma?

IDA. Fine. How was the war?

HENRY. It made me think.

IDA. Mr. Rothman was always thinking. He never

ate enough.

HENRY. Neither did you. *(He and IDA laugh.)*

ALICE. Show Henry the swing. *(MRS. PATTERSON pulls her hair.)*

HENRY. I've brought you these presents. *(IDA doesn't reach for them.)*

IDA. Oh! May we go out to the swing?

JUDGE. Hold on. Things are starting to get out of control here.

MRS. PATTERSON. How old are you, young man?

HENRY. Twenty-eight.

MRS. PATTERSON. My daughter is thirty-four.

JUDGE. What is your faith, Mr. Rothman.

IDA. He is a scientist.

HENRY. I am a chemical engineer, employed by the McKay Chemical Corporation in Appleton. My employers have told me that my future there is assured. Otherwise I would not have come.

I have great faith in the future of America. It is being formulated this minute in the laboratories of such forward-looking corporations as the one in which I am privileged to form a part. Some of the greatest minds in the country are gathering there.

IDA. I do not have a great mind.

MRS. PATTERSON. You do so. You graduated from the Milwaukee Normal School, didn't you?

HENRY. The cast of your mind is as fine as the delicate beauty of your hair. I would buy you silk pillow covers to prevent your curls from becoming unduly mussed in the night. *(Shocked gasps, sighs.)*

IDA. How do you know that?

HENRY. I have been researching the matter of women's needs.

JUDGE. I call that being forward, young man.

IDA. All scientists are, Father.

JUDGE. Pushy...

ALICE. I want to see the presents.

IDA. May I, Father?

JUDGE. Just one. *(IDA takes one of the gifts.)* I hate to think what it is. Let me open it. *(He takes the gift, unwraps it. A blue bottle.)* Perfume. Wouldn't you know it?

MRS. PATTERSON. Ooooooh. "Evening in Paris."

JUDGE. I'd say this is downright pushy.

MRS. PATTERSON. Ida is too young to wear perfume. *(IDA gives HENRY a look.)*

HENRY. Perhaps I can present this gift to you, ma'am.

MRS. PATTERSON. Well ... I *am* a married woman, so I guess it's all right.

ALICE. What's the other one?

HENRY. I'd rather give this to Miss Ida alone. My sisters send that to you. It was my mother's.

IDA. I'll open it myself, alone.

ALICE. What did you bring me? *(HENRY pulls out keys. Spins ALICE around.)*

HENRY. Perhaps you'd like a spin in my new car? Judge, maybe you can do the honors behind the wheel.

ALICE. Please, Father.

MRS. PATTERSON. Got your specks?

JUDGE. Yes. *(MRS. PATTERSON leads him and ALICE off.)*

Mrs. Patterson. Keep your eyes peeled for dogs and small children.

Judge. *(off)* She's not marrying a Jewish atheist. *(IDA unwraps her gift. It's a delicate old fan.)*

Ida. Oh ... Henry ... How lovely...

Henry. Keeps away the Moose Birds. *(They chuckle.)*

Ida. What a sweet smell it still has.

Henry. That was my mother's fragrance. She used to make sachets. Her room always smelled nice. She loved flowers.

Ida. So do I.

Henry. I thought so.

(They are about to kiss behind the fan when MRS. PAT-TERSON returns.)

Ida. Mama, look at this beautiful fan Mr. Rothman gave me.

Henry. Ma'am, I've seen a comfortable home in Appleton. It has a sundial, a birdbath, and a lovely garden ... and a sun room that would make a perfect nursery. I would get Ida a maid, when I could afford one. But in the meantime, I've seen a mechanical washtub with rubber rollers...

Mrs. Patterson. Ida, please return the fan to Mr. Rothman. And I will return to him this perfume. It is not seemly to keep presents from a young man if there is no hope for him here.

Ida. I love him.

Mrs. Patterson. She cannot have children. That is why she has not married.

IDA. I *can* have children. A child, maybe. I can have one.

MRS. PATTERSON. At the risk of your own life.

IDA. I would take the risk.

MRS. PATTERSON. Would *you*, Mr. Rothman?

HENRY. Ida will receive the greatest medial care in the country. Believe me.

IDA. I would like to stroll out to the swing now. With Henry.

(Before MRS. PATTERSON can object, IDA kisses her cheek. MRS. PATTERSON sighs, then puts a sun hat on IDA. IDA extends her hand to HENRY and they stroll away. We begin to hear music. The swing appears in a pool of light. There is a sense of branches and leaves. IDA sits on the swing. HENRY begins to help her swing gently back and forth. A young woman appears. She is IDA'S GRAND DAUGHTER. She looks at the figure on the swing.)

IDA's GRAND DAUGHTER. I remember an old photograph of my grandmother wearing that hat. I had a dream about it. Only in the dream I saw many women wearing it. And they were all sitting peacefully in a sunny place. Maybe a beach. I could hear music. The were humming something. Something beautiful. A waltz, I think.

(Magically, the pool of light expands to show MANY WOMEN surrounding IDA and HENRY, all dressed like IDA. They hum "The Missouri Waltz", swaying from side to side where they sit, as IDA continues to swing gently in the air.)

MUSIC CUE #13

SLOW CURTAIN

ACT II

ROSINA AND ALBERT (4)

MUSIC CUE #14

The attic of ALBERT's farmhouse before dawn. Cold wind screams around the eaves. ROSINA, 24 years-old now, enters carrying a lamp and her sewing box. She wears a robe. ROSINA goes to a trunk and lifts out her wedding dress, wrapped in layers of paper. She takes out large scissors.

LINDA, her 7-year-old, pushes open the attic door. She is in her nightgown and clutches the family doll.

LINDA. Don't cut up your wedding dress, Mommy!

ROSINA. What you doing up?

LINDA. You weren't in bed with Papa.

ROSINA. Didn't wake the man, did you?

LINDA. I thought it was a ghost walking around.

ROSINA. Just me. I'm the ghost in the attic.

LINDA. I'm cold. *(ROSINA puts arms around her.)*

ROSINA. You go back to bed. Go on now. You're a lucky little girl, Linda. Don't have to sleep with anyone. Got your own room. Shoot, I had to sleep with your Aunt Fanny, Angie Roo, Fay, Beulah, and the whole world. I never slept alone one night in my whole life.

LINDA. I love to hear stories about when you were growing up.

ROSINA. Not now, Sugar. I'll come down and crawl into bed with you when I'm done.

LINDA. Please don't cut up your wedding dress.

ROSINA. I'm going to transform this thing into the prettiest party dress you ever saw! The new train depot's opening up and your Aunt Fanny and her husband invited us to go. There's going to be a band and folks are coming from miles around. Folks who ain't seen me for years and years. And there's going to be all kinds of eats and dancing. Dances I probably don't know how to do. Mercy, I'm going to have to practice up on my dancing. Nothing like a party to make you improve yourself.

LINDA. Don't hurt your white dress.

ROSINA. Shoot, I'd rather dance the Missouri Waltz than keep an old wedding dress.

LINDA. Please...

ROSINA. Don't be a killjoy. Nothing worse in this world than a killjoy.

LINDA. I want it just like that when I get married.

ROSINA. Don't you want a store-bought one?

LINDA. No.

ROSINA. My, you have the saddest eyes I've ever seen. You were born serious. I don't know why. So serious about life all the time. *(Beat.)* You're right, Sugar. This bride's dress ain't mine no more. It's yours. I won't hurt it. See, I'll wrap it nice and put it away. I'll wear my black funeral dress. Look, Sugar, the sun's coming up. Don't know what I was thinking. I was even going to cut my hair and get my first permanent — yes, I was! Just 'cause I still got all my teeth I thought—

LINDA. Why doesn't Papa buy you a new dress?

ROSINA. I'm sure he would. But I don't want to trouble him, you know.

LINDA. I'll ask him.

ROSINA. No. He doesn't understand about women's things. He'll say the black dress is good enough.

LINDA. So you asked already.

ROSINA. Yup.

LINDA. Oh. Did you ask his permission about the wedding dress?

ROSINA. Sugar, the best thing to do with a man is just bite your tongue and do what you want. Or tell him how you feel and run for your life. *(They laugh. Suddenly LINDA puts a hand on ROSINA'S mouth. They listen.)* That your father walking around?

LINDA. Maybe he went for the strap.

ROSINA. It was just the wind. Sweetheart, I thank God for your company. Living so far out as we do, not seeing folks — you got to understand I grew up in a houseful of people. I miss my sisters so — you're my little sister, Sugar. I don't know if I'm bringing you up proper or not. Your Papa'd kill us if he knew we were jawing away up here. Look at these earrings, Linda. They're going to be yours when I die.

LINDA. Sometimes Papa gets so angry I think he's going to kill us all.

ROSINA. Ain't he fierce! Your Papa's a real man, Sugar. Mercy, no man in Iowa can fume like him. He's so hot inside that once when we were courting, a sofa we were sitting on started burning up! Mama blamed me for it and you Papa stuck up for me. Did I tell you he saved my life once?

LINDA. When you were on the railroad tracks and the train was coming?

ROSINA. Folks are still talking about it. He's a real life hero, Linda, except now he gets irritated easy 'cause his eyes don't see so good no more and his hearing's weak. Won't travel to where there's doctor's and hospitals.

LINDA. How'd the sofa burn up?

ROSINA. I don't know. Firecrackers most like. Angie Roo and Fanny Fern were always playing tricks. Let's go down.

LINDA. I don't want to go down.

ROSINA. Me neither. I'm so content.

(ALBERT'S footsteps are heard clearly.)

ROSINA. Put out the lamp, Sweetie.

(LINDA does. They huddle quietly, hearing the steps. The footsteps fade away.)

ROSINA. A man's got a right to kill his own family, you know. If that's the right thing to do.

LINDA. Is this a story or the real thing?

ROSINA. This is a real life story. You know my daddy, gentlest man on this earth. Well, when I was little, much littler than you, we heard a comet was going to come and crash into the earth.

LINDA. What's a comet?

ROSINA. A comet is a heavenly body. Halley's Comet it was called.

LINDA. Halley's Comet.

ROSINA. We knew the night it was coming, and everyone was so scared. Well, my daddy got us all together, Fanny Fern, Angie Roo, Fay and Beulah, and a big dog we had then. He put all the furniture in a circle and sat us down. He brought his shotgun in and said he'd rather put a bullet in each of us than have us suffer the poisonous gases the comet was bringing. First he was going to shoot the youngest, then the next, so on up to Mama, then himself. And we waited the whole night. We said prayers and sang hyms. Promised to see each other in heaven. When dawn came up — no comet. It just passed us by. So you, see, sometimes things look pretty serious — then, in the light of day, they're not so bad.

LINDA. I want you to have the dress. I think Papa will se you in it and it'll make him happy, remember his wedding day and have a good time. I'm going to be a nurse anyway and not get married. Then I can take care of Papa.

ROSINA. Are you sure? You won't cry when I start cutting it?

LINDA. I won't cry.

ROSINA. Better go down and not see me do it. If your Papa asks where we were, just say in the barn.

LINDA. Okay. *(She starts to go. ROSINA makes the first cut and LINDA begins to sniffle.)*

ROSINA. Sweetheart, why are you crying?

LINDA. I don't know. *(She goes. ROSINA continues to sew through the first part of the next scene.)*

(CROSSFADE)

MARGARET (3)

MARGARET has just finished a new poem.

MARGARET.
"...For the heart was made for loving.
   It's griefs must soon be spent;
Young hearts will go a-roving,
   Young lips will give assent."

"You will know again spring gladness,
   Summer-ecstasy, perchance.
Young hearts were made for madness,
   And youth is for romance."

(CROSSFADE)

ROSINA AND ALBERT (5)

*ALBERT enters, getting dressed for the dance. He practices his
   calls, in high spirits.*

ALBERT.
"Do si do your corner
Mind your feet and don't you fall
Right hand to your partner

And right and left the hall."

"Now swing your partner
Now swing 'em one and all
Take your pretty honey
And promenade the hall."

(ROSINA enters in her party dress. She has changed her hair style and wears earrings. ROSINA looks what she is, a young woman in flower.)

ROSINA. Husband ... *(He is almost struck dumb by her attractiveness.)* Don't you see me? I wish your tired old eyes was better so you could see me. I'll get up real close. See?

ALBERT. I sees you. And I smells you.

ROSINA. So? Ain't you surprised? Husband! I'm waiting for you to toss a compliment my way.

ALBERT. You look too inviting by half. No man — young or old — will be able to keep his hands off you. *(She curtsies.)*

ROSINA. Thank you, kindly. Ain't you going to be the envy of the county, you doing the calling and me doing the dancing ... *(She spins around. He stops her.)*

ALBERT. With you? Those young bucks crowded up at the barber shop today, aching for women?

ROSINA. I'll put on my black dress.

ALBERT. We ain't going. *(LINDA and HER DAUGHTER, who clutches the family doll, sit downstage, watching.)*

ROSINA. Lots of folks aching to see us.

ALBERT. Are you talking back to me?

ROSINA. Got your boots nice and polished...

ALBERT. You work hard. I suspicion it might give you some enjoyment to read to me from scripture. *(Pause. ROSINA turns and goes to her room. She puts her head in her hands. We see her through the following.)*

LINDA. I could hear your Grandma crying through the door.

DAUGHTER. She didn't go to the dance, then?

LINDA. No, she didn't. All she said to me was, "I just keep my mouth shut. There's things I'd like to say. Lots of times I'd like to talk. But I don't."

It was an unfortunate marriage. Your grandfather was too old for her. Well, she didn't have to suffer long. She died not long after that. A ruptured appendix.

DAUGHTER. Who took care for you?

LINDA. I did.

ALBERT. Where's my tea?

LINDA. After your Grandma died I had to face him myself. *(LINDA leaves her DAUGHTER, approaches her father, hiding a book behind her back.*

ALBERT. What you doing in that attic? It's past your bedtime, daughter. Where'd that book come from? No more books in the house I said!

LINDA. I'm graduating from the eighth grade next month, Papa. I'd like to go to nursing school. I could drive into town with Aunt Fanny's husband.

ALBERT. You do just fine looking after me. Don't bite your lip. Go to bed.

LINDA. What if I don't want to? *(ALBERT slowly starts to take off his belt.)*

ALBERT. What did you say?

LINDA. I didn't say anything. One of the reasons Mama died was there was no nurse! *(ALBERT strikes the table with his belt.)* I'll go anyway. I'll run away.

ALBERT. Go on, then. Runaway. *(He strikes table repeatedly.)* Go. Run away from me. Go. Go. Go...

(He collapses on a chair at the table. Before our eyes, ALBERT becomes an old man.)

LINDA. Let's go visit your grandfather at the rest home.

DAUGHTER. He scares me.

LINDA. He can't hurt you now.

(LINDA is an adult now. She takes her DAUGHTER by the hand. The girl lets go of LINDA'S hand and stays outside, playing on the grass. LINDA carries a pillow.)

LINDA. Hello Papa. *(She helps him to sit in a comfortable position, placing the pillow behind his head, and straightens the blanket around his shoulders.)* Are they treating you all right? Want something to drink?

ALBERT. They don't clean the glasses. Your mother knew how to wash glasses. Never minded drinking from a glass your mother washed.

LINDA. I've got a job.

ALBERT. Thought you was married now.

LINDA. I am.

ALBERT. Who you marry?

LINDA. Kenneth.

ALBERT. That Holy Roller.

LINDA. He's a Mennonite.

ALBERT. Never liked them much.

(LINDA hears her DAUGHTER'S laughter outside.)

LINDA. My little girl's playing right outside the window. It's so sunny and all.

ALBERT. You kind of look like your mother. Big eyes. Remember her? *(LINDA looks over at ROSINA, who smiles at her.)*

LINDA. Shoot. I remember her laughing all the time.

ALBERT. What you up to? *(LINDA takes a hairbrush out of her purse, starts combing ALBERT'S hair.)*

LINDA. Working. I'm the head nurse in the operating room now.

ALBERT. You're always working. Well, I didn't want you to be lazy. Help around here's all lazy. Nothing's clean. Germs...

LINDA. How's the food here?

ALBERT. I was never fussy, *(LINDA laughs.)*

LINDA. You were mighty particular about eats as I recall.

ALBERT. Always ate what was put in front of me. *(Beat.)*

LINDA. I'm going to bring my little girl in to give you a kiss.

ALBERT. Bring me some cigars next time you come. And big matches. Hell with the rules around here. I got my own rules. Always lived a correct life. Except about one thing.

LINDA. The party.

ALBERT. Yeah. The Fourth of July festivities. Can't die without coming clean. I was courting your mama. And we were sitting outside on a sofa watching the fireworks. It was an old sofa, stuffing coming out, her people were poor. Well, I lighted up a cigar and the match set the thing on fire. And she was blamed. Rosina was blamed. But I did it. And I never owned up to it. I wanted to. But she died. And it was too late to ask her forgiveness. *(He takes her hand.)* Please. You're the only one I can ask now. I don't want to die unclean. *(Pause.)*

LINDA. Shoot. I forgive you. For everything. *(Pause.)*

(CROSSFADE)

HANNAH (2)

MUSIC CUE #15 (Same as MUSIC CUE #10.)

A Mennonite hymn. HANNAH has returned to Indiana after her voyage to Constantinople. She stands, a Bible open in her hand, preaching to a group of Mennonite couples.

HANNAH. Love bears all tings, believes all tings, hopes all tings, endures all tings. Love never ends.

So beautiful in God's sight is te loving union of husband und vife ... a home of love, of kindness und gentleness ... of much joy und happiness ... of comradeship ... of prayer und devotion to te Lord. A home ver husbands love vives und ver vives love husbands. Beautiful are life's companions in God's sight. Loving companions.

(CROSSFADE)

(HANNAH remains visible in silhouette during the following scene.)

MARGARET (4)

As the group of young Mennonites moves off. one of them covers her head with a shawl and becomes MARGARET, who enters a confessional and kneels.

MARGARET. Bless me, Father, for I have sinned. It has been ... two years since my last confession. These are my sins — my sin. I have a strong desire to have a child of my own. But the man to whom I have entrusted my flesh has stopped — neglects his duties as a husband. He will not impregnate me. I am confessing my husband's sin, not my own, ha. ha. Oh, dear. Is it possible to do that, Father? I do everything else for him, why not get him absolution as well? Ha, ha. No. I don't do everything for him. Any more. And as a consequence I strap his son, my stepson, too freely. Yes. I confess that. But I use the strap on myself saying, "Through my fault, through my fault, through my most grievous fault." But there is not rest, only exhaustion. It is the greatest sin in the world to give a woman merely a fleeting glimpse of glory. To taste that ecstatic feast. And be left ravenous for more, knowing it is so close at hand, in one's house! Oh, Father, I think I have committed the greatest sin of all, to surmount the man's own passion. But I am ravenous. Please, please, speak to him, in God's name!

(CROSSFADE)

HANNAH (3)

HANNAH wraps herself in a shawl and approaches the bank of a frozen river. She is filled with excitement, hopes no one is observing her. It is a bright, cold day.

HANNAH. Lord, here I am again vanting to get on te ice. I know vee ist forbidden to do ice dancing, but I got dis terrible vice to fly on te frozen voter. Vot a temptation you make for me. In all of Europe I ain't never seen noting as beautiful as dis quiet part of te river ven it is frozen in vinter. *(She puts one foot on the ice, slides it around with glee.)* Och! It is so much fun! Please, I go on te ice a little minute. No one ist vatching. Noting bad ist going to happen. You forgive me, ya? *(HANNAH cautiously steps on the ice, begins to skate, spreads her legs and spins, joyful.)*

JACK. *(Voice.)* No devil dancing, Hannah Vangger! *(HANNAH, shocked, almost falls. Scurries to a small island.)*

HANNAH. Who ist der?

(JAKE appears from his hiding place on shore. Two pairs of ice skates dangle from his shoulder.)

JAKE. You ist a sinner for sure. Joost like me.

HANNAH. Jake. How did you know I vos here?

JAKE. I been following you here since you come back from Constantinople.

HANNAH. Are you going to tell de elders dat I do some ice dancing?

JAKE. Come here to me.

HANNAH. Why?

JAKE. Today only I come to you. *(He attempts to walk out on the ice, slips, falls. He laughs, holds out ice skates to her. She cowers away to another island.)* I go to Minneapolis to buy ice skates for you. I buy skates for me. Vee go on te ice together.

HANNAH. You buy skates for *me?*

JAKE. I put te skates on Hannah's feet.

HANNAH. You forget your poor vife so fast.

JAKE. Vee been friends long time Hannah Vangger. Vhy you don't shake my hand at te funeral of my vife?

HANNAH. Your vife vos my friend. Because her life vos so hard, she ask me to tell her about my days in Constantinople. Und so she is cooking und vashing and I am telling her of te day I see te Sultan of Turkey pass by in his carriage. Ya, I be invited to go vit oder Americans to a balcony in his palace, und all us guests is given one cigarette vit te Sultan's monogram as a rememberance. Und I give te Sultan's cigarette to your poor vife. *(JAKE takes out rather smashed cigarette and holds it out in his palm.)*

JAKE. Dis von.

HANNAH. Dat von. *(Tears come into her eyes.)* My treasure. But I give to her. Und it make her happy a little minute, to dream of oder places. But I tell her it not so goot der. Because te vomen is treated like slaves. Und she say ... She tell me I should not have come back here. But I explain I discover America over der.

JAKE. How?

HANNAH. I take my meals in Constantinople at te YMCA. I meet many American sailor boys. I sell dem embroidery my refugee ladies make, for der moders und girl friends back home. Und I discover American boys is plenty unhappy ... because tey do not know about Got. So, I say, I better do my missionary vork back home.

JAKE. Ya. Because, maybe, it is time for you to be a vife.

HANNAH. Maybe dat, too.

JAKE. Have American boys of your own.

HANNAH. I live vit my broder William. I help him vit his children. Tey is goot, happy children. But so many oders, tey be born only for ter hands. Only to vork on der foder's farms. Your vife give you plenty children.

JAKE. But I know I make more. So I ask my vife, ven are tey coming to help me? Und she say tey are not coming. Ya. She ... dat voman tell me she vill not have more. Und she so young yet. Und she not only kill te new vons coming, she boil many rolls of fly paper in tea und serve me tea to drink. But she not kill me. I lock her in te shed vit her flypaper to keep her warm und she freeze. Ya ... ya.

(His hand closes around the cigarette.) **All my days I been a farmer. Twenty year. Und I never been a farmer von day. I do not vant to be a farmer. I open here a big shoe store. I vant to sell shoes.** *(He kneels at her feet.)* **Hannah, you understand my poor vife. Now, maybe, you understand** *me* **a little, ya? You help me, ya? Only a voman can do dat, you.** *(Beat.)*

HANNAH. No.

JAKE. Please, you can forgive Jake. You ist so close to Got.

HANNAH. No.

JAKE. You preach about marriage, but you know noting about marriage. You vish to be ordained minister, but you know noting.

HANNAH. You ain't a man. *(He looks up at her. Places his two hands on his throat.)*

JAKE. Ya ... ya ...

(Freeze. The lights change. They remain in a pool of light. WILLIAM enters wearing Mennonite hat, which he takes off.)

WILLIAM. Hannah, I go out vit Ernie und Frank to Jake's place. Hannah, vee is too late. Te poor man hang himself in te shed. *(HANNAH cries out in anguish.)* Hannah, vee pray, ya?

HANNAH. I ain't a Christian. I ain't a Christian.

(WILLIAM approaches HANNAH and JAKE. He puts his arms around both, bows his head. STEPHEN and KENNETH step forward.)

STEPHEN. Dad, why wasn't Aunt Hannah ordained?

KENNETH. I don't know. She chose not to. She didn't preach for many years.

(CROSSFADE)

MARGARET AND JACK (5)

Jack is with his Firehouse friends. Some are reading newspapers.

FIREMAN #1. Hey! Jack Sheehan. Your old lady's in the paper again.

FIREMAN #2. Here's her photo next to a poem she wrote. Won a contest or something.

FIREMAN #3. Listen to this: "If there be tender love and harmony..." *(Whistles, hoots of laughter.)*

JACK. Pipe down. Or you'll be laughing out the other side of your mouth.

FIREMAN #1. "If there be tender love..." *(JACK SHEE-HAN grabs his hat and storms out amid jeers.)*

(MARGARET, in the silence of her home, is reading the paper.)

MARGARET.
"If there be tender love and harmony
Between two persons such as you and me,

Then always, one is restless with the other gone.
But two may roam the earth to its farthest strand,
Never lonely, going hand in hand."

(JACK enters the house. She jumps into his arms, but he retreats from her.)

MARGARET. I've won First Place in the District Authors' Club Contest!

JACK. Making a laughing stock of me, you mean. Printing your feelings for others to piss upon. Clucking like a cuckoo bird in the henyard. You're doing too much of it. The scribbling stops now! ... Cluck-cluck-clucking.

MARGARET. Quiet. The boy's asleep.

JACK. Where's my bottle?

MARGARET. Let me take your shoes off. Got your slippers right here. *(She bends down to untie his shoes. He practically kicks her away.)*

JACK. Stay away.

MARGARET. I want you to be comfortable. Put your dirty shoes on the furniture. I don't care. I run a very comfortable establishment here. James knows that. We had the most peaceful suppertime. We had your favorite — cream of corn soup! We missed you, but ... Your son is very kind to me. He said ... *(She is suddenly overcome, but controls herself.)* ... He said I would always have a home with him. He's frightened you're going to leave. He overheard someone say we had the worst marriage in town.

JACK. What did you tell him? *(She brings over two glasses.)*

MARGARET. I told him: "The worst marriage is the one

that never takes place." That's an old family saying. *(JACK pours some liquor for himself.)* Aren't you going to pour me a drink?

JACK. I haven't sunk that low. You think I've no respect for you?

MARGARET. You've got a girl sleeps with you in the firehouse.

JAMES. *(Off)* Mommy? What's the matter?

MARGARET. Nothing, dear.

JAMES. *(Off)* Is Daddy home?

MARGARET. Daddy's home, darling. Go to sleep.

JAMES. *(Off)* Good-night.

MARGARET. Good-night.

JAMES. *(Off)* Good-night, Daddy. *(Slight pause.)*

MARGARET. He says good-night. Sleep with the angels.

JACK. I'm sorry, Margaret. I'm desperate, see.

MARGARET. I am, too. I love you.

JACK. I love Evalyn. Your sister's been dead for years, but I still love her. I've tried to love you, sister, but it's no soap. A pal of mine read in a book that the heaviest weight in the world is the body of a woman you no longer love. Not all my pals are ignorant bums. *(Pause.)*

MARGARET. I've started a collection of Hummel figurines. Mr. Ables is importing them from Germany now. I'd forgotten to tell you. We hardly ever have the chance to talk any more. Let me show you. *(She opens a small box. Unwraps a figure, hands it to JACK.)* I've bought two. They're my children. Little children playing instruments, accordians, cellos ... some day I'll have a complete orchestra.

JACK. You've been spending too much lately. *(She puts

Hummel figurine away, starts darning a sock.)

MARGARET. Oh, and you're going to have to leave some money for the spring water. The boy came today for the bottles. Darling, love is for adolescents, not married people.

JACK. You just said you loved me.

MARGARET. Well, that's a word you like. I am interested in your considerable lust. Not your love. My no. You are lusty enough to seed entire forests. You must be more generous with your health, my man.

JACK. Mother of God, you've gone looney. Everyone says you're different, and it's true. Even Father Dillon says to watch you.

MARGARET. I've let you put me in hell.

JACK. I'm getting out of here! *(He rushes into the street. She follows and yells after him.)*

MARGARET. My husband's not a man! I've married a man who's not a man! *(He rushes back.)*

JACK. Shut your trap! Want the neighbors to hear!? *(Clapping her hands, in rhythm, she sings.)*

MARGARET.

OH, I MARRIED A MAN
A LION WAS HE
BUT HE DIDN'T KNOW A BLESSED THING
ABOUT RESPONSIBILITY!

JACK. Get in the house!

MARGARET. You've got to earn the right to tell me what to do!

JACK. You're my property. Obey me!

MARGARET. I'll let you in on a big secret, sweet darling. I'M NOT YOUR PROPERTY. We're not even married.

Ladies and gents of Junction City, we ain't married!

JACK. Shut your trap. We're married for life.

MARGARET. The marriage ain't valid. It ain't. I took the sacraments with a mortal sin on my soul. We both went to confession and communion and accepted the sacrament of matrimony, but I was in the state of mortal sin the whole while. That's why the marriage won't stick, see. Darling one, I prayed your wife would die. I wanted Evalyn to DIE. So I could get you for myself! I prayed for that. I LOVED YOU SO MUCH I RISKED HELL for one moment in your arms, you foolish bastard. I risked hell for you and I'm burning up now. Christ! Jesus Christ! *(She rushes back into the house. He follows.)*

JACK. What are you going to do?

MARGARET. I hear if you make tea with flypaper, you die.

JACK. Please don't do that ... I'll ... do me duty ... I'll do it.

MARGARET. WE ARE NO LONGER MARRIED.

JACK. Oh, yes we are! *(Enraged, he sweeps her into the air in his arms — as he did on their wedding day. She screams out.)* Until the day Little James gets married. He grows up with a mother and a father. You gave me your word, woman.

MARGARET. Yes. *(Slowly, he allows her to descend, pressed close to him.)* I gave my word.

JACK. That's a good girl. *(JACK slowly kneels at her feet.)* I'll do me duty. *(There is a row of buttons up the front of MARGARET'S dress. Starting with the bottom button, he slowly goes up her body unfastening buttons slowly, one by one, as MARGARET speaks. She stands unmoving, staring forward.*

JACK undresses her until she is only in her slip. She is trembling slightly.)

   MARGARET.
"There is no other wall so high,
no other barrier so insurmountable,
as that between two people
who have lost the common touch.
Two people who have been as one...
who sit together silently,
close as love, but far apart...
as hate.
Whose words have become as blocks
fused into walls of misunderstanding,
shutting out the light."

   JAMES. *(A man now.)* Wake up, Mama! It's my wedding day!

MUSIC CUE #16

(JACK now takes the combs from her hair. It is long and tumbles down about her, giving MARGARET the appearance of madness. Her hair seems to have turned gray. JACK covers her naked shoulders with a large flowing comforter.)

   JAMES. Get dressed, Mama. Dad's already waiting for us in the car. You look so beautiful and elegant and aristocratic. I bought this corsage for you. It kind of goes with the color of your eyes. Don't crush it with your fur coat. I love the smell of this fur coat.

Don't forget your gloves. Now, you're not going to cry. You gave me your word. Be happy. Look what you've accomplished. I'm terrific. Because of you. You've been the perfect mother. Scout's honor. You'll always have a home with me, sexy. I give you my word. *(He disappears. JACK kisses MARGARET on the cheek, picks up his hat and goes. Beat. MARGARET, an old woman, cries out.)*

MARGARET. Where am I? Somebody call the Volunteer Fire Department, they'll know what to do.

(She starts wandering around. MARY JO, a teen-ager enters.)

MARY JO. Nana, what are you doing up?

MARGARET. I don't know where I am.

MARY JO. In our house.

MARGARET. What happened to my house?

MARY JO. You're living with us now.

MARGARET. When I woke up, I didn't know where I was. I felt so frightened. Are you my mother? You look like my mother.

MARY JO. Nana, I'm James' little girl.

MARGARET. James left me.

MARY JO. He's out. He and Mom went to a party. I'm babysitting you. Nobody's home.

MARGARET. We are. But this isn't my home.

MARY JO. You should go back to your room now.

MARGARET. Where are my Hummel figurines?

MARY JO. Let me take you back to your room. I'll put you to bed.

MARGARET. Let go of my arm! All my life people telling me what to do. Collecting those Hummel figurines was my own idea. They must be worth a fortune now. Somebody stole them. And I was going to leave them to you, Mary Jo.

Mary Jo. No one stole them. You can see 'em in your room.

Margaret. See him? He's come back? Mary Jo bless your heart. We didn't fight that much the first year. He must have remembered that. *(She becomes dignified once more and starts out slowly.)* I'll make him some cream of corn soup. He always told me my cream of corn soup tasted just great.

(CROSSFADE)

IDA AND HENRY (3)

HENRY is polishing his car.

Ida. *(off)* I'm coming, Henry.
Henry. Don't rush yourself, dear.

(IDA comes out, stops at the top of the steps, breathless, looking beautiful. She wears a summer hat and gloves.)

Ida. Today's the day, Henry.
Henry. Today's the day...
Ida. Today's the day you're going to teach me to drive your car. You're terrified, aren't you? I'll put cotton in my ears if you want to bark at me. In your whole life, you've never raised your voice to me.
Henry. Never had any reason to. My! Don't you

look pretty.

IDA. I bought this dress for the occasion.

HENRY. Who says dreams don't come true? *(He wipes his hands, walks over to her, gallantly extends a hand to her and helps her down the steps, while singing.)* "Have you ever seen a dream walking? Well, I have."

IDA. I'm so glad I bought these driving gloves. I'm perspiring so already. I know my hands are going to slip off the wheel.

HENRY. You'll do very well.

IDA. Can you hear my heart?

HENRY. It's always like that the first time. You're not nervous, Ida. You're eager. I felt the same the day I learned to ride a bicycle.

IDA. A pleasure denied me. I could barely manage roller skates. It's my ankles, they're so weak.

HENRY. There's nothing wrong with your ankles, far as I can see. *(Wolf whistle)*

IDA. Now stop that. It's too early in the day...

HENRY. You like it.

IDA. I do not! I am an old married woman with a grown daughter!

HENRY. She blushing...

IDA. I am not!

HENRY. I know my Ida. You eat it up.

IDA. I do not approve of dalliance in public. I hate such things.

HENRY. What's this on your pretty forehead? Purple letters. It says, "I am telling a lie."

IDA. If you must know, Henry Rothman, your flirting simply frightens me to death.

HENRY. Why? This is a new one.

IDA. I'm serious.

HENRY. All right.

IDA. Now that I'm the hag on the block I've come to the realization that—

HENRY. You look the same way you did the day I proposed.

IDA. So do you. Better, I think.

HENRY. We're late bloomers.

IDA. Well, I *do* work on my appearance. That's what I told Sally Jane before she went off to Milwaukee Downer. I said, "The best advice a mother can give you is: never take anything for granted. You have to *work* at keeping up your friendships, you have to *work* to keep your romances. And when you're married you have to *work* to keep up — *(starts laughing)* Oh, that was so funny, Henry...

HENRY. What???

IDA. About the bloomers ... *(Continues to laugh, tries to control herself.)* I will say that for you, Henry, you do make me laugh. Oh, dear, what was I saying?

HENRY. Something about feeling your age and realizing something now.

IDA. Oh, yes. I've come to the conclusion that *I* am the scientist in the house. I am totally objective about *you,* but when it comes to *me,* you have no objectivity whatsoever. You idealize me. I'm frightened to death of the day the veil of love drops from your eyes and you see me in all my imperfections.

HENRY. That day will never come.

IDA. It will today. *(Beat. He kisses her softly.)*

HENRY. Take my hand. Now. we'll just go down to the front of the car. First, I want you to look under the hood.

IDA. Can't we go out on the road? I'm dying to make it go backwards.

HENRY. Not quite yet. How *do* you see me? Objectively speaking?

IDA. You're a Hercules, that's all. Why do I have to look under the hood?

HENRY. If you're going to drive, you have to learn what makes a car operate. Now, there's a catch here under the nose of the bonnet, like so ... and the hood lifts. *(Lifts hood.)* Now, please look inside and I'll tell you how it works. *(Pause.)*

IDA. Yes, Henry?

HENRY. This is how it works. *(Speaks, looking into the motor.)* A man marries a woman and spends his life with her. He moves to a community and stays there, hoping to provide his child a semblance of stability. And he becomes an employee of a forward-looking corporation and stays there all his years, earning respect and advancement, expecting — not unreasonably — that his career will be crowned with a position of leadership. Enabling him ... enabling his knowledge ... the full force of his knowledge ... to bear fruit. I have been informed that the company in its wisdom has seen fit to bar me from my future. I was next in line. But I — Henry Abraham Rothman — was passed over. Without explanation. *That* is how it works. Apparently. *(He turns to IDA, takes her face in his hands.)* I am not a foolish man in your eyes ... though I may seem so to myself and others. Never, never did I dream that my domestic life would triumph so completely over my office life. Your remarkable tenderness is so much more necessary to me now. My home is my fruit. *(pause)*

IDA. And you don't even know me.

HENRY. You don't have to learn to drive any more, now that I ... won't be travelling as much as I expected...

IDA. What's this? It looks like my vacuum cleaner.

HENRY. The air hose.

IDA. And this?

(Lights begin to fade.)

HENRY. The carburator.

IDA. And this?

HENRY. The battery.

IDA. The air hose, the car-burator, the battery...

HENRY. Wait a minute. Let me tell you about the air hose.

(CROSSFADE)

SOPHIE AND OSCAR (3)

The middle of the night. LITTLE MICHAEL is in bed. OSCAR comes home, humming a tune under his breath. He passes LITTLE MICHAEL'S door.

LITTLE MICHAEL. Grandpa...

OSCAR. Little Michael ... You awake?

LITTLE MICHAEL. I was waiting for you, Grandpa.

OSCAR. That's nice. Here, shake my hand. *(They shake. LITTLE MICHAEL finds a quarter in his palm.)*

LITTLE MICHAEL. Oh. I got to wash my hand now.

OSCAR. Why? That's quarter's pretty clean. See, it shines.

LITTLE MICHAEL. Grandma says money's got germs.

OSCAR. I'll wash your hand. *(He spits into LITTLE MICHAEL'S palm. Takes out big handkerchief, rubs palm dry. LITTLE MICHAEL laughs, delighted and disgusted.)* You think this ain't sanitary? What about little animals. This is how they wash their hands.

LITTLE MICHAEL. "The Little Goat"! "The Little Goat"!

OSCAR. Oye, I had to open my big mouth.

LITTLE MICHAEL. Please, Grandpa.

OSCAR. Wait for Passover. That's when you're supposed to sing it, when the meal is over and everyone's sitting around, full of food, happy. Not in the middle of the night. The musicians' union would defintely frown. Rehearsing at night ... Oye...

LITTLE MICHAEL. I don't know it.

OSCAR. We gone over it twenty times, Kinder.

LITTLE MICHAEL. I don't know it like you. Every word.

OSCAR. He's an artist. Okay, what am I gonna get for working overtime?

LITTLE MICHAEL. A kiss.

OSCAR. Give me your cup, you can kiss later. *(Takes cup next to bed.)* What's in this?

LITTLE MICHAEL. Tea and strawberry jam. So I won't get a cold for Passover. Grandma said.

OSCAR. I got a better recipe: *(Pulls out a small bottle.)* tea and vodka. It's great. Kills germs, kills pain, kills everything. *(Pours, drinks.)* Excited about Passover, huh?

LITTLE MICHAEL. Grandma says her brother's coming from Kansas City.

OSCAR. Sam Simon, he's a big shot in meat.

LITTLE MICHAEL. His wife said she'd come, too.

OSCAR. That's Clara, oye gevalt. I suppose the other Simon brother's coming, too? Jerry ... *(says with LITTLE MICHAEL)* ... Canned goods.

LITTLE MICHAEL. I want your brothers to come too, Grandpa.

OSCAR. I got a problem with them. They been fighting a long time. Morry wants to spell Robins with one "b" and Phil says "no", Robin's got to be spelled with two "b"s. When we came to America we changed the family name from Rabinovich.

LITTLE MICHAEL. I don't like that.

OSCAR. We should have kept it. It means son of the Rabbi. You come from a very learned family, from my side.

SOPHIE. *(Off.)* Let the boy sleep.

OSCAR. Want some of this tea and vodka? It'll make you sing better. *(LITTLE MICHAEL sips.)* I'll let you in on a big secret. Little Michael, light of my life, I'm about to realize a life ambition.

LITTLE MICHAEL. What?

OSCAR. Over on Rice Street there's a bar called "The Idle Hour", with a platform for live music. I'm going to buy it. Don't tell nobody yet. Okay?

LITTLE MICHAEL. Okay, Grandpa. *(They shake.)*

OSCAR. Well, that's really something to sing about. Now I'll sing for you, honey.

LITTLE MICHAEL. Not too loud. Papa's got to go to work tomorrow.

OSCAR. My son, Cutie, the early bird. Okay, here goes. Ready? *(Sings.)* MUSIC CUE #17

ONE LITTLE GOAT, ONE LITTLE GOAT,
   MY FATHER BOUGHT FOR TWO ZUZIM.

LITTLE MICHAEL.

ONE LITTLE GOAT, ONE LITTLE GOAT.

OSCAR.

THEN CAME A CAT AND ATE THE GOAT

LITTLE MICHAEL.

MY FATHER BOUGHT FOR TWO ZUZIM.

ONE LITTLE GOAT, ONE LITTLE GOAT.

OSCAR.

THEN CAME

TOGETHER.

A DOG AND BIT THE CAT,
   THAT ATE THE GOAT

MY FATHER BOUGHT FOR TWO ZUZIM.

ONE LITTLE GOAT. ONE LITTLE GOAT.

SOPHIE. *(Off.)* Cutie's got to go to work tomorrow.

OSCAR.

THEN CAME A STICK AND BEAT THE DOG,
   THAT BIT THE CAT THAT ATE THE GOAT

MY FATHER BOUGHT FOR TWO ZUZIM.

ONE LITTLE GOAT. ONE LITTLE GOAT.

SOPHIE. *(Off.)* Oye, veismir!

OSCAR. Your turn.

MICHAEL.

THEN CAME A FIRE AND BURNED THE STICK,
   THAT BEAT THE DOG THAT BIT THE CAT
THAT ATE THE GOAT
   MY FATHER BOUGHT FOR TWO ZUZIM.
   ONE LITTLE GOAT. ONE LITTLE GOAT.

OSCAR. Hey, he's got a good memory! Some more?
(LITTLE MICHAEL nods enthusiastically.)

   TOGETHER.

THEN CAME THE WATER AND QUENCHED
   THE FIRE,
   THAT BURNED THE STICK THAT BEAT THE
   DOG
THAT BIT THE CAT THAT ATE THE GOAT
   MY FATHER BOUGHT FOR TWO ZUZIM.
   ONE LITTLE GOAT. ONE LITTLE GOAT.

SOPHIE. *(off)* Come to bed, Oscar.

OSCAR. Can I sleep here?

LITTLE MICHAEL. Sure.

OSCAR. Okay, here goes. *(Starts quietly, builds to crescendo. Goes fast — a tour de force.)*

THEN CAME AN OX AND DRANK THE WATER,
   THAT QUENCHED THE FIRE THAT BURNED
   THE STICK
THAT BEAT THE DOG THAT BIT THE CAT
   THAT ATE THE GOAT
MY FATHER BOUGHT FOR TWO ZUZIM.
ONE LITTLE GOAT. ONE LITTLE GOAT.

THEN CAME THE SHOHET AND SLAUGHTERED
   THE OX,

THAT DRANK THE WATER THAT QUENCHED
THE FIRE
THAT BURNED THE STICK THAT BEAT THE
DOG
THAT BIT THE CAT THAT ATE THE GOAT.
MY FATHER BOUGHT FOR TWO ZUZIM.
ONE LITTLE GOAT, ONE LITTLE GOAT.

THEN CAME THE ANGEL OF DEATH AND KIL-
LED THE SHOHET,
THAT SLAUGHTERED THE OX THAT DRANK
THE WATER
THAT QUENCHED THE FIRE THAT BURNED
THE STICK
THAT BEAT THE DOG THAT BIT THE CAT
THAT ATE THE GOAT
MY FATHER BOUGHT FOR TWO ZUZIM.
ONE LITTLE GOAT. ONE LITTLE GOAT.

THEN CAME THE HOLY ONE, BLESSED BE HE,
AND SLEW THE ANGEL OF DEATH,
THAT KILLED THE SHOHET THAT SLAUGH-
TERED THE OX
THAT BURNED THE STICK THAT BEAT THE
DOG
THAT BIT THE CAT THAT ATE THE GOAT
MY FATHER BOUGHT FOR TWO ZUZIM.
ONE LITTLE GOAT. ONE LITTLE GOAT!
(LITTLE MICHEAL applauds with glee.)
    CUTIE. *(Off.)* Pop, I'm going to kill you!

(OSCAR jumps into bed. He and LITTLE MICHAEL hide under the bed covers. Lights begin to fade.)

SOPHIE. *(Off)* You see, Oscar, you woke your son up.

CUTIE. *(Off)* He always does that.

SOPHIE. *(Off)* Don't cry, Cutie.

CUTIE. *(Off)* Mama, I'm going to call the cops!

SOPHIE. *(Off)* Oh, I'm going to hit him. I'm going to hit him. Oscar, Oscar!

(CROSSFADE)

HANNAH (4)

HANNAH is sitting outdoors. A quilt covers her legs, her Bible on her lap. She uses a large handkerchief because she has a cold.

STEPHEN enters, carrying a colorful motorcycle helmet at his hip.

STEPHEN. Hi, Aunt Hannah. *(He kisses her.)*

HANNAH. My Hell's Angel.

STEPHEN. Mom said to bring you inside.

HANNAH. Ugh! She is too old-fashioned, your moder.

STEPHEN. How was California?

HANNAH. Too many nuts collect out der by te ocean. I miss te cold. *(Sneezes, blows her nose.)* I ratter freeze dan shiver.

STEPHEN. *(Imitating.)* Vell, you sountet like you always had a colt anyway.

HANNAH. Oooooh. I'm going to pull your ears! You bat boy.

STEPHEN. I am a bad boy.

HANNAH. Not vorse dan me. My moder, she give me eggs in a basket to sell at te store. I am such a careless girl two eggs roll out of te basket and break open! Och. Vat suffering. I hide te eggs under a fence.

STEPHEN. That's nothing. What about the slaughter of the watermelons.

HANNAH. Och! You and your broders were so terrible! Your poor Foder...

STEPHEN. Poor Foder...!

HANNAH. He had a garage full of votermelons. And you bat boys use a hatchet and break tem up!

STEPHEN. Dad broke us *up*.

HANNAH. But I do something much vorse.

STEPHEN. Yeah, what?

HANNAH. I am crossing te ocean to Constantinople. You know I go der?

STEPHEN. Who doesn't? You get this free trip and...

HANNAH. I go der for Christ. Americans is going to Cuba and te Philippines fighting und killing in te name of Manifest Destiny! Und vee go in te name of peace. In te name of love!

STEPHEN. So what did you do that was so bad? You were saying that when you vos crossing te ocean...

HANNAH. Ya. I go to te railing and toss my black Mennonite bonnet overboard. It vos a goot day for a toss.

STEPHEN. That is bad. I won't tell anybody.

HANNAH. Nobody ashamed about anyting any more nowdays. Ven vee vos bat my foder discipline us in a "symbolic" vay. But choost as painful. Ya.

STEPHEN. Symbolic?

HANNAH. He vos so strict. He say — "Go outside und get a lettuce leaf." Und vee get de lettuce and give to him und he vood say, "Bent over" und hit us. *(Tears come to her eyes.)* Te pain ... te shame vas so bat.

STEPHEN. I have to confess something to you, Aunt Hannah ... in my way — so I want us to be mature about the way we handle this — cool. I don't want you to start preaching to me, singing one of your hymns about the Holy Spirit! God! Why did you have to come back. All it took was having you sleeping in the house again for me to start having nightmares.

Okay. Okay. One of the things that makes us different is that we don't get baptized until we're old enough to choose baptism out of some personal conviction. Wait till people grow up and feel a sincere conversion to Christ. I waited a long time. And I appreciate your coming all the way back from California to be here when I was baptized. Aunt Hannah, I didn't feel a sincere conversion. I shouldn't have gone through with it. But I thought that the moment I was baptized I'd suddenly feel what you do — a connection with God. But I didn't. Aunt Hannah, I have no faith. I don't believe. I thought when I was baptized I would understand ... I don't. I don't understand.

HANNAH. Do you understand *me?*

STEPHEN. *(Quietly)* No.

HANNAH. Do you love me?

STEPHEN. Yes.

HANNAH. Dat is enough. Dat is enough. Dat is plenty. To feel love...

STEPHEN. I was so worried. It was as if your whole life meant nothing to me.

HANNAH. Your vay vill be different, dat is all.

STEPHEN. Did you tell your mother you broke the eggs?

HANNAH. Ah ... I could not sleep. So ... I got up and vent to tell her.

STEPHEN. What did she do?

HANNAH. She kisst me und said, "Now you can sleep." *(She looks at STEPHEN, then takes his face in her hands and kisses his forehead.)* Now you can sleep. *(Pause.)* I have von request.

STEPHEN. Name it.

HANNAH. You let me put on dat pretty hat. *(He places the motorcycle helmet on her head. She is thrilled.)* I feel like te first lady astronaut.

STEPHEN. I better take you inside now. *(He picks her up in his arms.)*

HANNAH. My body is stopping, but my mind is not.

STEPHEN. You want a ride on the back of my motorcycle?

HANNAH. Oooooooo...! I put on my slacks.

STEPHEN. I think we could manage it, when your cold gets better. *(They start out.)*

HANNAH. I never did get a chance to vatter ski in California.

(CROSSFADE)

TRANSITION

MUSIC CUE #18

In dim light, while humming a Hebrew song, the entire company sets up a Passover table. This is done by placing a bench across two other benches. This is followed by the placing of a tablecloth, plates, flowers. Finally, the candles are lighted. The group stands around the table until the song ends, then, everyone disappears except LITTLE MICHAEL.

SOPHIE AND OSCAR (4)

Passover. Festive candles on the dining room table. LITTLE MICHAEL is seated there alone, singing quietly to himself.

Little Michael.
"ONE LITTLE GOAT, ONE LITTLE GOAT,
MY FATHER BOUGHT FOR TWO ZUZIM..."

(AUNTIE CLARA enters.)

Clara. Oh, look at the table. It's beautiful. Look at the table, Little Michael.

Little Michael. I'm looking.

Clara. Isn't it beauiful? *(Screams out.)* Sophie, the table looks beautiful. Only good things can happen on Passover. Why you sitting here all by yourself, honey?

Little Michael. I'm hungry.

CLARA. Where's your grandfather, sweetie?

LITTLE MICHAEL. Papa and Mama are looking for him.

CLARA. You're a lucky little boy to be living with your grandmother.

(SAM enters.)

SAM. Why's he lucky?

CLARA. Sam, sit down and shut up.

SAM. My sister is a witch.

CLARA. A house ain't blessed without a grandmother in it. *(beat)* Cutie and his wife are very lucky. They don't have to pay a babysitter.

SAM. Clara, go help Sophie in the kitchen.

CLARA. She's had everything prepared for days. You know her.

SAM. Then why don't she come out?

CLARA. Change the subject. *(Indicates LITTLE MICHAEL.)* De kind...

(JERRY enters carrying a football.)

JERRY. I been looking for you, Little Michael.

LITTLE MICHAEL. Yes, Uncle Jerry? *(JERRY smashes the football into MICHAEL'S stomach.)*

JERRY. Do Sophie and Oscar sleep in the same bed?

CLARA. Jerry, for God's sake!

LITTLE MICHAEL. Yes.

JERRY. The kid's lying.

SAM. Our sister is a martyr.

JERRY. Clara, Oscar's got a girl. They play duets together.

CLARA. Don't talk dirty in front of the boy.

JERRY. He don't understand. You don't understand, do you, Cutie?

LITTLE MICHAEL. Cutie's my father.

JERRY. Oscar's got two homes. He can't afford one and he's got two. He keeps her in a room above Mother Merrill's.

SAM. It's the Robin's Curse.

LITTLE MICHAEL. Mother Merrill's is Grandpa's office. He takes me there.

JERRY. You hear that?

LITTLE MICHAEL. What's the Robin's Curse? *(Dead silence.)*

CLARA. Your grandmother's wine is delicious.

SAM. You aren't supposed to drink it yet.

(Sophie enters.)

SOPHIE. Okay. Let's start.

LITTLE MICHAEL. I want to wait for Grandpa.

CLARA. It ain't Passover without the master of the house.

SAM. My sister is the master of house.

SOPHIE. Little Michael's hungry. Let's start.

SAM. You love Little Michael more than your own brothers.

LITTLE MICHAEL. What's the Robin's Curse?

SOPHIE. Don't worry. You don't got it. You ready to ask the four questions?

LITTLE MICHAEL. Yes. Why is Grandma a witch? *(Beat.)*

SAM. Sometimes she's a witch, sometimes she's a martyr.

CLARA. Your grandma tells fortunes, honey. That's what he meant.

SAM. The Robin's Curse means that if you got Robin's blood you'll turn out lazy, a soft touch, no good, a musician, not a merchant, not American, not able to buy anything...

LITTLE MICHAEL. Grandpa's going to buy a bar. On Rice Street. I saw it.

SOPHIE. What?

LITTLE MICHAEL. It's got a name: *"The Idle Hour."*

JERRY. Figures.

SAM. How's he going to pay for it?

LITTLE MICHAEL. The man at the bank said it was okay because we have a house.

SOPHIE. He mortgaged the house!

LITTLE MICHAEL. I shouldn't have told.

CLARA. We'll talk later. Now we got to get this dinner over with. So, let's start. Okay, who can read?

SAM. I'll do the honors.

CLARA. Skip a little.

SAM. Before we start, I just want to say that it's a blessing only Simons are here tonight. We are a loving family. And I think we're going to end up having a peaceful Passover for a change.

SAM. *(Reads.)* "Baruch atoh adonai elohenu melech ho'olom boray p'ri ho-adomah." *(They drink wine. SAM dips parsley in vinegar, passes it around.)* "Baruch atoh adonai elohenu melech ho'olom boray p'ri ho-adomah." *(SAM breaks matzah in two, holds up the matzah plate.)* "This is the bread of affliction which our forefathers ate in the land of Egypt. All who are hungry — let them come and eat. All who are needy — let them come and celebrate the

Passover with us. Now we are here; next year may we be free men." *(Puts down plate; second cup of wine is served.)* The questions will be asked by the youngest person present.

LITTLE MICHAEL. *(reads haltingly)* "Why is this ... night ... different from ... all ... other nights?"

(OSCAR enters.)

OSCAR. I'm so sorry to be late.

SOPHIE. Go on, Little Michael, honey.

OSCAR. Sophie, I gotta talk to you a moment.

SOPHIE. Where's Cutie?

OSCAR. Helping the guests off the truck.

SOPHIE. What guest's?

OSCAR. I didn't catch all their names. They don't speak English too well. *(Everyone goes to peer out a window.)*

CLARA. What? Immigrants? Refugees? Displaced Persons?

SOPHIE. Oscar Robins, you love everyone in the whole world except me.

JERRY. Cutie's bringing 'em in!

LITTLE MICHAEL. I'm frightened, Grandma.

SOPHIE. It's okay. They can come in, but the drum player goes. For keeps.

OSCAR. *(Indicating people outside.)* Sophie, I brought you a Passover present...

SOPHIE. Some present. You never gave me one thing in my life I wanted. You want to give me something? I'll tell you what I want. I want a divorce from you.

OSCAR. Okay. I'll go. See you tomorrow.

SOPHIE. No. Don't go, if you're not going forever. Go. Get out. Go with your girl to "The Idle Hour"!

MUSIC CUE #19

(OSCAR looks at LITTLE MICHAEL who runs off crying. Lights dim to darkness as VOICES form part of a magical, musical transition.)

VOICE. Little Michael ... where are you?
VOICE. Michael Harry Robins ... come home.
VOICE. Come back...
VOICE. Michael...
VOICE. Come back...

(VOICES begin fading and we begin to see a million stars in the night sky.)

VOICES. *(sung)*
MICHAEL ... MICHAEL ... MICHAEL...

(MICHAEL is discovered sitting up in a tree, contemplating the night sky. SOPHIE comes out wearing her apron, humming her Yiddish lullaby.)

SOPHIE. Too bad Michael's run away. I baked his favorite poppy seed cookies.
MICHAEL. Here I am, Grandma. I was talking to the stars.
SOPHIE. I heard you calling.
MICHAEL. I've been thinking about you since you died.
SOPHIE. How are my tulips?
MICHAEL. I don't know. They sold the house.
SOPHIE. Honey, what do you want?
MICHAEL. Talk.
SOPHIE. With you, my grandson, I could talk. Not with anyone else.

MICHAEL. Did you really love Grandpa? *(Beat.)* I gotta know. *(Beat.)*

SOPHIE. Yeah.

MICHAEL. I'm glad you came.

SOPHIE. Is something wrong?

MICHAEL. Oh, I've just been thinking about a lot of important things now that I'm getting married.

SOPHIE. Married! My grandson is getting married! A nice Jewish girl, yes. *(Beat.)*

MICHAEL. Uh ... Her grandparents came from Ireland, I think. Sheehan.

SOPHIE. Irish?

MICHAEL. Uh-huh.

SOPHIE. The lost tribe. So, it's okay. You're gonna have a nice, big wedding, yes?

MICHAEL. We've got school friends coming from all over the map: from Junction City, Iowa; Appleton, Wisconsin, Minneapolis...

SOPHIE. What's her name?

MICHAEL. Mary.

SOPHIE. Miriam.

MICHAEL. Mary Jo. Sheehan.

SOPHIE. Oh, so American.

MICHAEL. She is.

SOPHIE. You love this girl?

MICHAEL. Yes. She needs love real bad. I sense it's always been in short supply around her house.

SOPHIE. It's important for you to know, sweetie, we got a strong chain of love ain't been broken — from my great-grandfather to you. And your grandfather's people — oye! Maybe they had too much love.

MICHAEL. Grandma — it's ... unbearable for me ... not having you and Grandpa at the big days in my life. You won't be at my wedding.

SOPHIE. *(Beat.)* If *you'll* be there, *I'll* be there. *(Beat.)* We'll all be there. The whole family.

(Beat. MARY JO appears in a pool of light. She is ready for her wedding in a simple, white, high-waisted dress, a delicate garland of spring flowers in her hair.)

MICHAEL. That's Mary Jo. *(He goes to MARY JO, takes her hand. They walk into a pool of light in the center of the stage.)*

(Circling them appear the PERSONS of the play. We hear music. MICHAEL and MARY JO join hands, look at one another.)

HANNAH. So beautiful in God's sight is te loving union of husband und vife ... a home of love, of kindness und gentleness, of much joy und happiness. Beautiful are life's companions in God's sight. Loving companions.

(The music continues as...)

MUSIC CUE #20

THE CURTAIN FALLS

PERSONAL PROPERTY PLOT

(All properties should be carried on except those pre-set before the start of Act Two.)

ACT ONE

Prologue
Linda:

    Kitchen matches

Scene One — Rosina and Albert (1)
Rosina

    Stylized horse's head held by Rosina that ties
        around her waist with leather thongs. (Not essen-
        tial, if the director decides to mime the horse.)
    Stick of licorice — in her pocket

Albert

    Large key ring that hooks to his belt with lots of
        keys
    A cigar and matches

Scene Two — Margaret and Jack (1)
Jack

    Small bottle of liquor
    A penknife
    Carries on potato from off stage

Casey

    A gun

Margaret
> Carries on a parlor lamp
> Writing portfolio with papers inside
> A pen

Scene Three — Rosina and Albert (2)
Albert
> A cigar and matches
> A chair
> Wrapped box containing an alarm clock
> Folded paper — the lease for the back of the
> barber shop

Rosina
> Pillows

Rosina's Father
> Box of fireworks

Angie Roo and Fanny Fern
> Both carry trays with "eats" — cookies

Rosina's Granddaughter
> An old family doll

Rosina's Mother
> A box of snuff

Scene Four — Ida and Henry (1)
School Children
> May carry on parts of the classroom, as desired,

such as, an American flag, a recess handbell, a globe of the world, a goldfish bowl.

Girls
>Little apple juice glasses

Chee Chee
>Smelling salts

Scene Five — Sophie and Oscar (1)
Sophie
>Materials needed to make egg noodles — dough she can pound, rolling pin. Strips of wet wool can serve to represent already made egg noodles that Sophie hangs on back of chair

Oscar
>Since he is a drummer, actor may choose to carry a pair of drumsticks in his pocket, which he can pull out and use any time he wants for emphasis
>
>A quarter (25¢) in his hand
>
>Smashed tulip in jacket pocket
>
>A big paper bag that contains: a pair of B.V.D.'s and a chicken

Scene Six — Albert and Rosina (3)
Albert
>A baby coffin
>A hammer

Rosina
> A mug of warm milk

Scene Seven — Hannah (1)
Hannah
> A Bible
> A heavy suitcase

Scene Eight — Margaret and Jack (2)
Jack
> Wedding bouquet

Margaret
> A white carnation

Fireman
> Old fashioned gold firehose nozzles. (The archway of water can be done in many ways. In the first production at the Illusion Theatre, Minneapolis, seltzer water bottles were used. In the Pittsburgh Public Theatre production, buckets filled with paper streamers were used. Or, the action can be mimed.)

Townswomen
> Rose petals

Scene Nine — Sophie and Oscar (2)
Sophie
> Sabbath candles
> Matches

Rosina
> Needle and thread (mimed)

Oscar
> Small painting of radishes

Scene Ten — Ida and Henry (2)
Judge Patterson
> Newspaper

Children
> A ball

Henry
> Two wrapped gifts: a blue bottle of perfume,
> "Evening in Paris", and an antique fan
> A calling card
> Car keys

Mrs. Patterson
> Carries on sun hat and hat pin for Ida later in
> the scene

Alice
> Cloth for drying plate
> A plate

ACT TWO

(Pre-set: a trunk that contains a wedding dress wrapped in layers of paper, and old earrings; also, a quilt on a chair used in the nursing home scene by Albert.)

Scene One — Rosina and Albert (4)
Rosina
> A lamp (could be the same one used by Margaret in Act One, Scene Two)
>
> A sewing box that contains large scissors; later sewing, use of needle and thread, can be mimed.

Linda
> The family doll

Scene Two — Margaret (3)
Margaret
> Her writing portfolio
> A pen

Scene Three — Rosina and Albert (5)
Linda
> A book
> Carries pillow to nursing home (Pillow could be inside trunk.)
> Hairbrush inside purse (See costume plot.)

Scene Four — Hannah (2)
Hannah
> Her Bible

Scene Five — Margaret (4)
> Rosary

Scene Six — Hannah (3)
Jake
        Two pairs of ice skates

William
        Optional—covers Jake's shoulders with a quilt

Scene Seven — Margaret and Jack(5)
Firemen
        Newspapers

Margaret
        Newspaper
        Bottle of liquor and two glasses, carries on from off
            stage pantry
        Hummel figurine (could be inside trunk)
        Sock (From inside her pocket); needles and thread
            could be mimed

Jack
        Large, flowing comforter to cover Margaret, which
            he gets from off stage or is pre-set

Scene Eight — Ida and Henry (3)
Henry
        Cloth to polish car (Could simply be his hand-
            kerchief or mimed)

Scene Nine — Sophie and Oscar (3)
Little Michael
        A cup (of tea and strawberry jam)

Carries on bedcovers or quilt

Oscar
>   A quarter (25¢) in hand
>   In jacket pockets: drum sticks, big handkerchief,
>   bottle of vodka

Scene Ten — Hannah (4)
Hannah
>   Her Bible
>   Quilt to cover legs
>   Large white handkerchief

Stephen
>   Carries motorcycle helmet (See costume plot)

Scene Eleven — Sophie and Oscar (4)
Entire company
>   All help to set up Passover table: tablecloth, plates,
>   wine glasses, ingredients for the ceremony, can-
>   dles, Passover readers....

Jerry
>   A football

Entire company
>   For transition in darkness: everyone can create the
>   stars by lighting pin-flashlights, lighting them one
>   by one and moving them slowly in circular arcs.
>   Or, stars can be created by lighting a match off
>   stage to the tips of long punks; a group of punks
>   held in each actor's hand produces many tiny
>   orange stars.

COSTUME PLOT

(Since the actors play a variety of roles, they should wear a basic cos-
tume with add-ons and take-offs. In a few cases, such as Ida and
Henry in their last scene, the actors should wear different clothing to
show the passage of time. Below are listed the essentials needed for
dramatic effect.)

ACT ONE

Scene One — Rosina and Albert (1)
Townspeople at railroad track

> The company is discovered in their basic outfits.
> Women in long skirts, blouses, shawls, maybe a
> basic pinafore or two, or a bonnet. Men in shirt
> sleeves, trousers, some suspenders, vests, one in
> coveralls.

Rosina

> Underdrawers

Albert

> As the most prosperous man in town wears pants,
> shirt, cravat, vest, jacket, hat
>
> Large key ring that hooks to his belt with lots of keys
> (See property plot)
>
> Important transition note: At end of scene he changes
> his hat for another hat when he becomes another
> character in scene two. This lets the audience know
> right away that actors will be playing multiple roles

Scene Two — Margaret and Jack (1)
Firemen
>A couple wear colorful, old-fashioned firemen's
>hats, if possible.

Jack
>A mourning band on his jacket sleeve
>A hat
>A tie

Margaret
>A lilac-colored, lacey peignor that trails behind
>her

Scene Three — Rosina and Albert (2)
Abby
>Pregnant stomach

Scene Four — Ida and Henry (1)
School children
>Maybe boys roll up their sleeves and girls wear rib
>bons in their hair

Ida
>Midi blouse
>Large bow gathers her curls at the nape of her
>neck

Henry
>World War I uniform — putees on lower legs
>Soldier hat

Scene Five — Sophie and Oscar (1)
Sophie
    Colorful apron
    Colorful scarf

Oscar
    Tuxedo

Scene Six — Rosina and Albert (3)
Albert
    In shirt sleeves
    Suspenders

Rosina
    Robe

Scene Seven — Hannah (1)
Hannah
    Mennonite cap
    Dark outfit
    Dark stockings
    Dark shoes

Mennonite hymn singers
Men
    Wide-brimmed black hats, if possible

Women
    Dark bonnets, if possible

Kenneth
>   Mennonite hat
>   Vest

Stephen
>   Mennonite hat
>   Vest

Scene Eight — Margaret and Jack (2)
Jack
>   As before, but truly looks dashing: hair combed,
>   boots polished

Margaret
>   White lace mantilla on head
>   Wedding outfit could be a dark lilac suit, white
>   blouse with ruffles at the neck

Firemen
>   Old-fashioned fire hats, if possible

Father Dillon
>   Priest's cassock

Townspeople
>   As festive-looking as possible

Mary Jo
>   Teen-ager look: bobby-sox, pony tail, sweater

Scene Nine — Sophie and Oscar (2)
Sophie
>   No apron
>   Gold earrings
>   Lace mantilla

Oscar
>   Carries jacket
>   Sleeves rolled up

Scene Tem — Ida and Henry (2)
>   Judge Patterson
>   Sweater
>   Glasses

Henry
>   Good suit
>   Hat

Mrs. Patterson
>   The most affluent older woman in play thus far,
>   wears:
>   Shawl
>   Necklace
>   Earrings

Alice
>   Midi blouse
>   Pigtails

Ida
    Pastel-colored summer dress
    Bow at nape of neck
    Sun hat, later in scene

Women in dream (All the women in the cast)
    Sun hats

ACT TWO

Scene One — Rosina and Albert (4)
Rosina
    Slip
    Robe or quilt

Linda
    Nightgown

Scene Two — Margaret (3)
Margaret
    Wedding outfit without jacket

Scene Three — Rosina and Albert (5)
Albert
    Big belt
    Nursing home sequence, covers himself with pre-
        set quilt

Rosina
    White party dress made from wedding dress. This

is usually achieved by simply removing a lower
layer of the wedding dress, making it look
shorter.

A white flower in her hair
Earrings

Linda

Becomes adult in nursing home sequence by putting on high heels
Purse with hairbrush inside (See property plot)

Scene Four — Hannah (2)
Hannah

As before

Scene Five — Margaret (4)
Margaret

Shawl (to cover head)

Scene Six — Hannah (3)
Hannah

Shawl

Jake

Dark Mennonite trousers, vest, jacket, hat

William

Mennonite hat

Scene Seven — Margaret and Jack (5)
Margaret

Dress that buttons down the front
Slip
Large, flowing comforter (See property plot)

Mary Jo
Teen-ager outfit as before

Scene Eight — Ida and Henry (3)
Henry
1940's tie
Sweater
Glasses

Ida
1940's summer dress
Hat
Gloves
Purse

Scene Nine — Sophie and Oscar (3)
Little Michael
Pajamas

Scene Ten — Hannah (4)
Hannah
Shawl
Glasses

Stephen
Motorcycle helmet (See property plot)
Leather jacket
Jeans

Scene Eleven — Oscar and Sophie (4)
Little Michael
     A yarmulka on head
     Pullover
     When older, puts on jacket for wedding

Auntie Clara
     Dressy outfit
     Jewelry

Sam
     Yarmulka on head
     Suit

Jerry
     Yarmulka on head
     Suit

Sophie
     Her dressy sabbath outfit
     Apron

Mary Jo
     Wedding dress: simple, white, high-waisted
     Delicate garland of spring flowers in hair

Company
     Characters as couples appear at the wedding
       dressed in the costumes they wore at the mo-
       ment of their greatest happiness

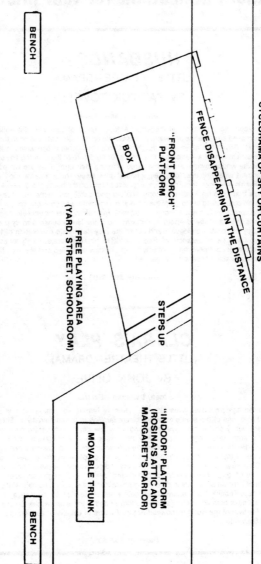

BENCH

CYCLORAMA OF SKY OR CURTAINS

FENCE DISAPPEARING IN THE DISTANCE

"FRONT PORCH" PLATFORM

BOX

FREE PLAYING AREA
(YARD, STREET, SCHOOLROOM)

STEPS UP

"INDOOR" PLATFORM
(ROSINA'S ATTIC AND
MARGARET'S PARLOR)

BENCH

MOVABLE TRUNK

FLOOR PLAN
BECOMING MEMORIES

Other Publications for Your Interest

HUSBANDRY
(LITTLE THEATRE—DRAMA)
By PATRICK TOVATT

2 men, 2 women—Interior

At its recent world premiere at the famed Actors Theatre of Louisville, this enticing new drama moved an audience of theatre professionals up off their seats and on to their feet to cheer. Mr. Tovatt has given us an insightful drama about what is happening to the small, family farm in America—and what this means for the future of the country. The scene is a farmhouse whose owners are on the verge of losing their farm. They are visited by their son and his wife, who live ''only'' eight hours' drive away. The son has a good job in the city, and his wife does, too. The son, Harry, is really put on the horns of a dilemma when he realizes that he is his folks' only hope. The old man can't go it alone anymore—and he needs his son. Pulling at him from the other side is his wife, who does not want to leave her job and uproot her family to become a farm wife. *Husbandry*, then, is ultimately about what it means to be a *husband*—both in the farm and in the family sense. *Variety* praised the ''delicacy of Tovatt's dialogue'', and called the play ''a literate exploration of family responsibilities in a mobile society.'' Said *Time*: ''The play simmers so gently for so long, as each potential confrontation is deflected with Chekhovian shrugs and silences, that when it boils into hostility it sears the audience.'' (#10169)

(Royalty, $60–$40.)

CLARA'S PLAY
(LITTLE THEATRE—DRAMA)
By JOHN OLIVE

3 men, 1 woman—Exterior

Clara, an aging spinster, lives alone in a remote farmhouse. She is the last surviving member of one of the area's most prominent families. It is summer, 1915. Enter an immigrant, feisty soul named Sverre looking for a few days' work before moving on. But Clara's farm needs more than just a few days' work, and Sverre stays on to help Clara fix up and run the farm. It soon becomes clear unscrupulous local businessmen are bilking Clara out of money and hope to gain control of her property. Sverre agrees to stay on to help Clara keep her family's property. ''A story of determination, loyalty. It has more than a measure of love, of resignation, of humor and loyalty.''—Chicago Sun-Times. ''A playwright of unusual sensitivity in delineating character and exploring human relationships.'' —Chicago Tribune. ''Gracefully-written, with a real sense of place.''—Village Voice. A recent success both at Chicago's fine Wisdom Bridge Theatre and at the Great American Play Festival of the world-reknowned Actors Theatre of Louisville; and, on tour, starring Jean Stapleton. (#5076)

(Royalty, $50–$35.)

Other Publications for Your Interest

SEASCAPE WITH SHARKS AND DANCER
(LITTLE THEATRE—DRAMA)

By DON NIGRO

1 man, 1 woman—Interior

This is a fine new play by an author of great talent and promise. We are very glad to be introducing Mr. Nigro's work to a wide audience with *Seascape With Sharks and Dancer*, which comes directly from a sold-out, critically acclaimed production at the world-famous Oregon Shakespeare Festival. The play is set in a beach bungalow. The young man who lives there has pulled a lost young woman from the ocean. Soon, she finds herself trapped in his life and torn between her need to come to rest somewhere and her certainty that all human relationships turn eventually into nightmares. The struggle between his tolerant and gently ironic approach to life and her strategy of suspicion and attack becomes a kind of war about love and creation which neither can afford to lose. In other words, this is quite an offbeat, wonderful love story. We would like to point out that the play also contains a wealth of excellent *monologue* and *scene material*. (#21060)

(Slightly Restricted. Royalty, $50–$35.)

GOD'S SPIES
(COMEDY)

By DON NIGRO

1 man, 2 women—Interior

This is a truly hilarious send-up of "Christian" television programming by a talented new playwright of wit and imagination. We are "on the air" with one of those talk shows where people are interviewed about their religious conversions, offering testimonials of their faith up to God and the Moral Majority. The first person interview by stalwart Dale Clabby is Calvin Stringer, who discourses on devil worship in popular music. Next comes young Wendy Trumpy, who claims to have talked to God in a belfry. Her testimonial, though, is hardly what Dale expected . . . Published with *Crossing the Bar*. (#9643)

(Royalty, $15.)

CROSSING THE BAR
(COMEDY)

By DON NIGRO

1 man, 2 women—Interior

Two women sit in a funeral parlor with the corpse of a recently-deceased loved one, saying things like "Doesn't he look like himself", when the corpse sits up, asking for someone named Betty. Who is this Betty, they wonder? God certainly works in mysterious ways . . . Published with *God's Spies*. (#5935)

(Royalty, $15.)

Other Publications for Your Interest

A WEEKEND NEAR MADISON
(LITTLE THEATRE—COMIC DRAMA)
By KATHLEEN TOLAN

2 men, 3 women—Interior

This recent hit from the famed Actors Theatre of Louisville, a terrific ensemble play about male-female relationships in the 80's, was praised by *Newsweek* as "warm, vital, glowing . . . full of wise ironies and unsentimental hopes". The story concerns a weekend reunion of old college friends now in their early thirties. The occasion is the visit of Vanessa, the queen bee of the group, who is now the leader of a lesbian/feminist rock band. Vanessa arrives at the home of an old friend who is now a psychiatrist hand in hand with her naif-like lover, who also plays in the band. Also on hand are the psychiatrist's wife, a novelist suffering from writer's block; and his brother, who was once Vanessa's lover and who still loves her. In the course of the weekend, Vanessa reveals that she and her lover desperately want to have a child—and she tries to persuade her former male lover to father it, not understanding that he might have some feelings about the whole thing. *Time Magazine* heard "the unmistakable cry of an infant hit . . . Playwright Tolan's work radiates promise and achievement." (#25051)

(Royalty, $60-$40.)

PASTORALE
(LITTLE THEATRE—COMEDY)
By DEBORAH EISENBERG

3 men, 4 women—Interior
(plus 1 or 2 bit parts and 3 optional extras)

"Deborah Eisenberg is one of the freshest and funniest voices in some seasons."—Newsweek. Somewhere out in the country Melanie has rented a house and in the living room she, her friend Rachel who came for a weekend but forgets to leave, and their school friend Steve (all in their mid-20s) spend nearly a year meandering through a mental landscape including such concerns as phobias, friendship, work, sex, slovenliness and epistemology. Other people happen by: Steve's young girlfriend Celia, the virtuous and annoying Edie, a man who Melanie has picked up in a bar, and a couple who appear during an intense conversation and observe the sofa is on fire. The lives of the three friends inevitably proceed and eventually draw them, the better prepared perhaps by their months on the sofa, in separate directions. "The most original, funniest new comic voice to be heard in New York theater since Beth Henley's 'Crimes of the Heart.'"—N.Y. Times. "A very funny, stylish comedy."—The New Yorker. "Wacky charm and wayward wit."—New York Magazine. "Delightful."—N.Y. Post. "Uproarious . . . the play is a world unto itself, and it spins."—N.Y. Sunday Times. (#18016)

(Royalty, $50-$35.)